Treasurer's

and

Controller's

Letter

Book

Treasurer's
and
Controller's
Letter
Book

JOEL J. SHULMAN

Prentice-Hall, Inc.
Englewood Cliffs, N. J.

Prentice-Hall International, Inc., *London*
Prentice-Hall of Australia, Pty. Ltd., *Sydney*
Prentice-Hall of Canada, Ltd., *Toronto*
Prentice-Hall of India, Private Ltd., *New Delhi*
Prentice-Hall of Japan, Inc., *Tokyo*

Library of Congress Cataloging in Publication Data

Shulman, Joel J
    Treasurer's and controller's letter book.

    1. Commercial correspondence. 2. Form letters.
3. Accounting. I. Title.
HF5726.S478   651.6'5   73-12360
ISBN 0-13-930552-1

Printed in the United States of America

About the Author

Joel J. Shulman is presently Senior Editor for Magazines for Industry, New York City, where he writes articles on financial and managerial aspects of business operation. He has also served as consultant to business on key questions involving fiscal and corporate affairs. The author has been in the financial and marketing communications field for a total of 20 years. During this time, he has held management posts for industrial and commercial companies in such specialties as financial and technical writing, advertising, public relations, communications and marketing services.

Mr. Shulman's articles on financial, general management and marketing communications have appeared in a variety of magazines, including *Business Management, Industrial Marketing, Science and Technology* and *Electronic Design.*

The author has taught communications and technical writing at the New School for Social Research and at Bronx Community College. He holds B.S. and M.A. degrees and is currently a Ph.D. candidate.

Mr. Shulman is a senior member of the Society of Technical Writers and Publishers and the Technical Association of the Pulp and Paper Industry (TAPPI).

How This Book Will Help You Write Better Letters that Get Things Done Effectively

How much time does it now take you to write the difficult letter, the letter that determines whether your company is respected in its financial relations or merely tolerated?

How much "brain-racking" do you have to do to write the letter that you may need only once in awhile, but that must be written *exactly right* to obtain the results you want to achieve?

How much time do you spend on letters that should be routine but that take inordinate amounts of time for checking, rewriting and rework, even though they could actually be written by your secretary with proper verbal instructions?

To meet the unusual, to meet the difficult, to meet the day-to-day situations, you need letters that quickly get to the point, make no unusual commitments, are gracious and courteous, explicit and definitive and, most importantly, get the results you want. How do you know you can achieve all these objectives? Simply follow the more than 300 model letters and alternate phrasings of the letters in this book.

Using other peoples' knowledge and experience can cut your letter-writing and dictation time to a fraction. Most of the letters you need for your work have been written before. These are the letters you need to handle more than 90 percent of your letter-writing chores. The other letters that you need only when your company has made new fiscal arrangements are much more difficult to write, yet they too have already been written for you.

Sometime, somewhere in the course of your work, you may have to face an unusual situation that calls for some special correspondence. You may have a new type of business venture or a new business situation, or you may have a difficult personal situation involving your work. How should you approach these situations? It is easiest to rely on other peoples' experience in these matters, and it is easy to follow their examples.

The model letters you will find here are the "first-class" examples that were used in real-life business situations. *Every single letter*—without exception—*comes from an actual company and was used in actual correspondence.* They were specifically selected by chief fiscal officers *from their own files* as representing those letters that they found most effective—letters they spent many hours polishing, until they were certain that they achieved the absolute optimum in results. Since all individuals are different, you will probably want to tailor your letters to suit your own personality and the personality of your company.

These are actual letters, not made up ones. They come from some of the world's largest companies, as well as from small and medium-sized companies. They come from industrial companies, retail organizations, utilities, and even from the New York Stock Exchange. They have been collected from vice-presidents of finance, treasurers and controllers. Each major contributor admitted that he could have used some standard letters if he had had them; now, you can.

A poor letter may cost your company thousands of dollars, and you may be using a poor letter right now! Compare what you have been using to these superior specimens and see where you can improve your company's correspondence with your very next letter.

You will save invaluable time when you select the model letter that comes closest to your immediate requirements. Just imagine the time you'll save when you tell your secretary to use selected paragraphs, adding only the name of the addressee or your company name. You will save time to enable you to do the work of greatest value to your company, and your correspondent will still get a personal letter. You can increase your dictating speed, get to the subject faster and easier—just by following the patterns established in the model letters.

Coverage of letters in this book is broad. You'll have letters concerning bank dealings, dealings with auditors, security exchanges and the Securities and Exchange Commission. You'll find ways to parry requests from security analysts, refuse credit to poor risks and present your case for better credit consideration. Shareholders, insurance company personnel and employees must get letters. And, to meet the demands of the infrequent but critical mergers, acquisitions, changes in corporate identity and other dynamic situations, you'll find letters to cope with these types of situations. Each letter is a model of legally sound and crystal-clear communication.

You will find a wide variety of very-hard-to-write letters, such as a covering letter with a check to the beneficiary of a recently deceased employee, or, another on how to graciously refuse the request of a security analyst who wants to tour your company's facilities at a time when he knows you may be planning a public stock offering.

Some books on letter-writing tell you what to do in a given situation. Others have many hundreds of so-called "letters," which are really compilations of what the authors believe would be the most effective letters for a situation, but which, nevertheless, are still only guesses. This book is truly unique: it gives you the *actual words to use* when you face a fiscal crisis—the precise words that have already been used where they were measured in actual dollars and cents.

Sometimes the words are not the nicest, but they are effective, having been proved in actual situations. This book is free from preaching, free from theories of correspondence and grammatical rules, free from useless explanations. It is hard-headed, practical, direct—from the people who face letter-writing situations every working day of their lives. Every letter is shown in its entirety. Every letter has been selected from among many others on the same topic—all to provide you with the finest specimens available.

Here are some of the letters you will find:

On page 142 is a letter enclosing a check to the widow of a company executive who just died. How do you express your condolences, yet attempt to compensate in some financial way for the loss of a loved one? It can be done; just follow the model letter.

An entire section is devoted to letters affecting mergers. If you have policies on extending credit that differ from the merged company, how do you make your requirements known? And what about changes in name to reflect changed scope of business? You'll find letters on these topics on pages 130 and 136, with alternate wordings that you may find more appropriate to your own situation.

Do you write an effective collection letter, or do you find that your company is sending out letters that may be insulting but not effective? Some companies get poor results while others do quite well. There are several collection series given in Group B, each letter well-honed, each series appropriate for a given situation.

Turning down security analysts without fear of future loss of good relations is easy with the letters in Group D. The analysts will thank you for your courtesy.

Save company time and money with letters that refuse contributions (page 163); refuse to contribute effort to non-productive activities (page 167); refuse to commit the company to continuing projects that could drain financial resources and manpower (page 162).

Forms Used in Place of Correspondence

A great deal of numerical data is transmitted by fiscal officers through the mails. Much of this data is not capable of being reduced to verbal form suitable for standard correspondence; it must stand in much the same manner as a conventional set of accounting records. In addition to numerical data, formal reports are sent, reports that follow prescribed formats and are the substance of the transmittals. The letter that is written serves more as the proof of the transmittal having taken place than as an informative document in itself. It would contain no information about the substance of the matter it discusses.

Forms are used for claims for damages; fiscal data concerning earnings, profits and taxes; requests for insurance to be paid for losses incurred; credit information; activities related to banking; legal matters, and many, many more purposes. Should we have attempted to show all the possible forms that a controller uses or could use, we would fill what has already proved to be a complete and sizable library of forms. Letters used to cover transmittal of forms generally follow a pattern in which reference is given to a case, file or company number or account; the text confirms the substance of the enclosure and the sender closes his letter. Only in certain rare instances does the covering letter go into further detail. These instances are so infrequent as to constitute very special conditions, which either are not likely to be met in the normal course of the work of a fiscal officer or truly call for special letters.

Telegraphic Communication

Night letters, telegrams, TWXs, cables, and other transmittals are similar in form and style and are presented in letter form. All may be used for a variety of reasons, some of which include:

1. The need to establish, without doubt, the time and date of transmittal.

2. A confirming record of the contents is needed and this record is held by a disinterested party.

3. Speed of transmittal with a permanent record is required.

Years ago, when the likelihood of mail being delivered was so close to 100% that the exceptions did not matter, the existence of a postmark on an envelope was proof of the time and date of actual posting. This presumed several factors, which were: the letter was mailed before the time of the postmark; the postmark was legible; the envelope was preserved along with the contents and was filed with the correspondence. None of these conditions hold true in present business practice. With the advent of postal meters, it is entirely possible to falsify the date of transmittal or to have the envelope bear an erroneous date. Errors of date-changing, which occur in all business offices with meters, are so frequent that postal officials have had to become more lenient in accepting dated mail. What happens, in such a situation, is that the meter is not turned to the correct date until several (or more) pieces have passed. As a result, the date that appears on these few envelopes posted through the meter early in the day cannot be trusted.

The matter of legibility is another area of concern. Some postmarks simply are not legible. Sometimes—and increasingly so—letters are delivered without ever having been postmarked, either because they slipped behind other letters or because the marking machine missed them completely. Therefore, there is no assurance that a usable postmark will appear on an envelope.

As for preserving the envelope, this was fine when mail was not opened and sorted by a mail clerk who discarded the envelopes. Discarding of envelopes can cause serious embarrassment, as when an envelope from a Spanish-speaking country is discarded and the letter itself bears no name of country of origin. If you were to receive a letter from San Benito or Santa Cruz, it is impossible to know the country of origin without either the postmark or the postage stamp itself. Of course, an order received in an envelope that was discarded is worthless.

The need for a confirming record is another problem area compounded by poor postal service. Since the postal record is not reliable, some other means must be found to establish a legal date. The use of telegraphic communication solves this problem. A certified or registered letter might also serve the purpose, but not if speed is desired. A night letter or telegram provides absolute guarantee of overnight service to any point in the world. No postal system can do as well.

Although a night letter, telegram, cablegram or other telegraphic communication will be much more terse than a formal letter, it will contain the same type of information. If reference is needed, it will be so stated at the outset. The subject matter will be stated completely, but without certain grammatical form and social amenities, which make letters easy-flowing in their literary style. The closing is without cordiality. Since the recipient of such a communication is aware of the need and desire for brevity, he accepts the form of the "letter" in good grace; he is not insulted if the style is terse and even ungrammatical (to a certain extent, that is). However, the message should not become distorted or ambiguous for reasons of poor grammar. The few extra cents it costs to clarify a message is well worth the cost to avoid complications at a later date.

Virtually none of the letters shown here ever requires telegraphic transmittal, although the several letters that might be transmitted in that manner are so indicated.

The Telephone and Other Non-Written Communications

An unusual approach to communication is taken in this book. As a special bonus feature, there is an entire section devoted to communication by use of the telephone.

Any description of the communications needs of treasurers and controllers must take into account the importance of the telephone, a medium without equal to perform certain limited functions. It can serve as an aid in avoiding legal and other entanglements that might ensue from use of written communication, particularly in exploratory stages of negotiations. Because of the need for controllers and treasurers to avoid committing their companies to fiscal arrangements that may become embarrassing, the telephone is a very useful instrument when used properly.

Increasingly, the telephone is used to make preliminary loan arrangements, to avoid the embarrassing "dunning" letter to previously excellent paying customers, to plead for time to repay obligations whose due dates are threateningly near, and for other negotiations where the tone of a person's voice can convey "information" and attitudes. The telephone is also useful when making early contact to "sound out" the respondent, with the letter to follow confirming the contact and refining the general discussion to specific terms. It can be wide-ranging without being committal; it allows certain ineptitudes without making either party confirm his ignorance. It preserves pride until it is necessary to make a firm commitment.

Written communications are sometimes best avoided as a means of preserving the privacy of information. A new, recent awareness of the need for security involves not only the protection of property but the protection of records from damage, destruction or from unwanted prying. Discussions concerning actions in progress, where written records are not absolutely required, should normally take place orally. In the past, this would have been done easily, but the national scope of business now demands a different method of discussion. Only those persons who are privy to such information would then have such knowledge. Nevertheless, the final communication would probably have to be put into written form.

Specific details of how to use telephone contact or the need to avoid written contact are given in the last chapter of the book. This bonus feature is unusual in a book on writing letters, but since this is a unique book, it covers the full spectrum of "communications," not just of the act of writing letters.

There are times when the security of the written communication versus that of oral communication must be weighed, one relative to the other. This book helps you make decisions with assurance. Prying occurs with oral contact as well as with written contact, and the limitations of each method of conveying unambiguous information have to be judged against the merits in each individual case.

JOEL J. SHULMAN

Acknowledgments

Many corporate fiscal officers took the time and effort to respond to my requests for letters that would serve as samples for their colleagues. I owe sincere thinks to and gratefully acknowledge the assistance given to me by the following individuals:

L. A. Orlando, Controller, Andy Gard Corporation

Carl A. Herold, Treasurer, Breeze Corporations, Inc.

David W. Foy, Controller, Alsar Manufacturers, Inc.

Henry L. Brown, Vice-President, National Distillers and Chemical Corporation

Gerald A. Parsons, Director of Financial Relations, Champion International Papers, Inc.

Julian A. Altman, Treasurer-Controller, Spiegel

Merle S. Wick, Vice-President, New York Stock Exchange

W. M. Butler, Vice-President–Treasurer, Chatham Manufacturing Company

Stanley Rosch, Senior Vice-President & Controller, Castle & Cooke, Inc.

James J. Wainscott, Controller, American Rubber and Plastics Corp.

Peter J. Gagnot, Vice-President–Finance, Narda Microwave Corp.

Stanley A. Kaplan, Controller, VISIrecord Systems Division of Barry Wright Corporation

E. C. Papke, Credit Manager, Questor Corporation

John A. Abbott, Manager Line Services, Dresser Crane, Hoist & Tower Division of Dresser Industries

Frederick J. Hetzel, Treasurer, Dow Jones & Company, Inc.

John M. Emery, Assistant Vice-President and Assistant Treasurer, Columbus and Southern Ohio Electric Company

Howard E. Sabin, Treasury Staff, The Foxboro Company

Donald M. Woodard, Publisher, Management Accounting magazine

G. R. Martin, Division Controller, Robertshaw Grayson Controls Division

Joe M. Shaver, Manager Personnel & Administration, Exxon Corp.

James T. Murphy, Controller, Frontier Airlines, Inc.

Victor Karpf, Controller, Greenwald Industries, Inc.

W. G. Hand, Vice President, Houston Natural Gas Corporation

Henry G. Wetter, Vice President and Controller, The Guardian Life Insurance Company of America
George Shenitz, Certified Public Accountant, New York, N.Y.
J. M. Stokes, Vice President and Secretary, Gulf States Utilities Company
Wm. Dean Ankrum, Controller, Meredith Corporation

*C*ontents

How This Book
Will Help You
Write Better Letters

7

GROUP A

Relationships with
Banks and Bankers

23

GROUP B

Credit Situations
Involving Customers

45

GROUP E

GROUP F

GROUP G

GROUP H

GROUP I

✿ ✿ ✿ ✿ ✿

group A

RELATIONSHIPS WITH
BANKS AND BANKERS

Relationships with Banks and Bankers

Since controllers and treasurers are involved primarily in matters concerning money, they deal with banks and bankers a good deal of the time they spend at work. Many of the transactions involving banks are no more involved than a household checking account, and dealings in such instances are on a routine basis. Yet even this routine involves correspondence, some of it establishing only the fact that documentation is created to provide a basis of action acceptable in law. The existence of "a piece of paper" is all that is required to verify actions taken.

Despite the knowledge that each particular letter is absolutely necessary to have on record, the contents of each letter should bear close similarity to a prescribed format. What might appear a minor point, optionally included, could turn out to be a pivotal point in a legal situation. Omissions cannot be tolerated if they refer to changes of conditions and authorizations. For instance, to add a power of attorney for a corporate officer who has replaced one who has retired and to fail to indicate the removal of the power of attorney of the retired person could result in a bank's honoring a signature that is no longer valid. More important, if retirement was forced, the still-valid power of attorney might one day "haunt" the company.

These are situations that cannot be handled verbally, although some of the prior negotiations might be initiated and carried to conclusion in conversations, meetings and even luncheons. Nevertheless, they cannot be formalized and acted upon until some formal written notice is provided.

As with dealings with all business associates, letters are needed as matters of courtesy. There is truly no substitute for the "thank you" note; it is a bit of old-fashioned courtesy that does not go out of style. Written matter has a certain warmth because of its permanence that spoken material can never hope to achieve.

Because of their many special dealings with bankers, treasurers and controllers cannot possibly cover the scope of correspondence with "conventional" letters. A situation may be unique for a corporate officer and for his company. It may recur within a short time or it may never happen again. Letters written on such occasions cannot serve as examples. These are the letters that must be written with the greatest care; they are worthy of the time and thought they require.

1. Covering Letter for Line of Credit with Collateral Attached

Applications for loans are accompanied by some statement of the collateral offered, whether a personal loan or a loan requested by a corporation. In this example, the collateral is a promissory note bearing the full faith and credit of the corporation and properly executed by duly authorized corporate officers. Any collateral could be offered that would be legal and would be acceptable to the lending institution: other corporate securities, mortgages, etc. All that is necessary is that the collateral be negotiable.

As with any loan, some limitation is set for the amount of the loan. With a corporation, the authorization for the loan must also be stated. If the authorization is contained in other documents, such as the minutes of the meeting of the Board, they must be provided to the bank for their records.

General Approach

Terms and conditions are stated concerning the application. All specifications are stated, including, as noted, dates of various actions taken. This particular letter, from a regulated public utility, indicates that they will accept—and probably have been offered—the prime interest rate prevailing at the time they offered their note. Other corporations may not be as fortunate and the interest rate would necessarily be stated in no uncertain terms.

The authorization for the loan is stated as being an action taken at a meeting of the board of directors. Since banks do not normally wish to lend money that is placed on deposit for demand accounts at other banks, it can be assumed that prior negotiations have taken place and that it has been agreed upon as to how the proceeds of the note will be transferred. The action of transferring the loaned funds to another bank is as much a part of the total transaction as is the application for the loan itself. Whether the sum is in the tens of dollars or millions of dollars, the notification of completion of the transaction is sent by the bank to the account holder.

model letter A.1

Dear Mr._____:

We hereby apply for a loan of $2,500,000 under our line of credit with your bank. Our promissory note dated January 9, 19___ for that amount is enclosed. The note is for a ninety day term and is to bear interest at your best rate in effect on January 9.

The aggregate borrowings to and including the date of this loan are $12,836,000, which is not in excess of the $40,000,000 authorized by our Board of Directors on April 5, 19___.

Please credit the proceeds of the note to our account in your bank, forwarding **(a)** your usual advice to us.

Also, on the morning of January 9, 19___ please transfer by bank wire the sum **(b)** of $2,500,000 to our account at the _____ National Bank of _____.

Sincerely,

ALTERNATE WORDING

Except insofar as the proceeds of the loan are to be transferred to another bank, the basic approach is suitable for most purposes. Only the numbers, dates, and specific terms and conditions would be changed to suit any other particular situation.

(a) Please credit the proceeds of the note to our account, forwarding your advice to us. By your acknowledgment, please confirm the amounts, rates and terms of all of our outstanding loans as of the date of your response.

(b) Thank you for your attention to this matter of importance to us.

2. REQUEST TO BANK TO GRANT A NEW LINE OF CREDIT WITHOUT INDICATION OF COLLATERAL TO BE OFFERED

Arrangements for credit are normally handled on a direct, personal basis before any formal correspondence is initiated. Formal correspondence is required to enable both sides to work within an established framework after the initial conditions have been thrashed out. Normally, such initial conditions go further than a mere statement of desire on the part of one party and agreement on the part of the other party; they actually go so far as to indicate the amount of credit to be extended and the terms and conditions that would likely be acceptable to both parties. It is with regard to the early discussions that the first paragraphs of both this and the next letter are framed. Reference to such prior discussions is the first item mentioned.

General Approach

This type of letter would be used where the borrower is not already doing business with the lender. Information is given to assure the lender that his funds will be in the hands of a well-managed company, a company that already enjoys the confidence of many of his colleagues. It is a request for the issuance of a completely new line of credit from a new lender.

The second paragraph provides the reason for wishing to have a new line of credit and the assurances to the lender of how the credit would be used. The nature of the commercial paper is not indicated and may not be presumed. Therefore, the strength of the corporate borrower is more important than the type of paper he will offer as collateral. Since it is not possible to issue paper without proper backing, the line of credit must be opened first, and that is precisely what has been asked for—no more. If more definite information can be given at this point it should be, unless it involves a disclosure that may be contrary to regulations governing such disclosures.

The third paragraph states the amount desired. It could stand separately or as part of the second paragraph.

The closing allows for the possibility that, having had no previous association with the borrower, the banker may wish to prolong the negotiations until all his doubts are laid to rest.

model letter A.2

Dear Mr. Cromwell:

As Frank Smith has discussed with you, we are interested in increasing our banking lines of credit. At present, the Company has a formal credit agreement with 12 major banks totaling $40 million. In addition, we have informal lines of $20 million with the same banks.

It is our desire to increase our informal line by $40 million, thus bringing the total ABC Company lines to $100 million. These additional lines would initially be for the purpose of backing up Commercial Paper, which we may be issuing in the next year or so. Thus, we would not anticipate calling on them in the immediate future.

Therefore, we are requesting XYZ Bank to consider extending us a $3 million informal line of credit. We would expect that this line would be subject to review on an annual basis.

If you have any further questions on this request, feel free to call Frank or myself. I am looking forward to hearing from you shortly on this matter.

Very truly yours,

3. Request to Bank to Expand an Existing Line of Credit Without Indication of Collateral to be Offered

When compared to the letter requesting credit from a new lending institution, this letter is rather informal. It can be used when the relationship between lender and borrower has already proved comfortable for both parties and where each party enjoys the confidence of the other.

General Approach

Less information is needed where the company has a line of credit already in existence and wishes to augment the line by an amount stated to cover additional contingencies that are considered likely to arise. As the letter indicates, the request is for an extension of an existing line of credit.

Terms and conditions that may be expected to be attached to the line of credit are indicated, even in such an informal letter. This is necessary because all parties to the ultimate transaction cannot rely upon the informal oral representations given to them by other persons. They may not doubt the accuracy of such statements, but neither would they have the assurance that comes directly from the borrower, and in writing on his own letterhead, concerning his intended use of the funds and his assurances of periodic review by the lender.

The closing presumes upon the existing relationship and asks only for confirmation of the arrangement. There is, however, no automatic presumption that the arrangement will be approved, although that may have been part of the prior informal discussions. There is no reason why the closing could not indicate some feeling on the part of the writer that this arrangement will prove mutually satisfactory. A closing of this sort could be used in place of the more cautious tone of the sample letter.

model letter A.3

Dear Don:

Frank Smith and I enjoyed the opportunity of joining you and Dave Yelton for lunch last Friday.

As we discussed, we are interested in extending our lines of credit. In addition to our present lines, it is our desire to obtain additional lines totaling approximately $40 million. These would be used primarily for the purpose of backing up Commercial Paper, which we may be issuing in the next year or so.

Therefore, we are requesting the Bank of America to consider extending us a $5 million informal line of credit. We would expect that this line would be subject to review on an annual basis.

I am looking forward to hearing from you again on this matter.   **(a)**

Sincerely,

ALTERNATE WORDING

(a) May I hear from you favorably about this matter soon.

or . . .

I trust this arrangement will prove to be to our mutual benefit.

4. REQUEST FOR TEMPORARY EXTENSION OF EXISTING LINE OF CREDIT DUE TO RUN OUT

Credit levels required by a company fluctuate widely. Seldom does a controller or treasurer wish to keep open a line of credit and pay the interest when he has no immediate use for the money. A simple letter asking that the credit be renewed is all that is necessary, and the action takes only a day. Here, as in all dealings with banks involving the credit of the company, the formal letter represents the results of prior negotiations. Without the letter, no transaction can be consummated, for it alone commits both parties.

General Approach

A request for extension of a line of credit is simply and solely that. A borrower—a company in this case—asks for money to be made available for its use on an open-account basis, without collateral. Interest rates that have been agreed upon should be restated in the letter or, as in this case, established against an accepted standard.

model letter A.4

Dear Mr._____

We are enclosing a copy of our 19___ annual report for your files in connection with our line of credit with your bank.

Would you please confirm extension of the line to April 30, 19___, in the amount of your legal limit, which according to our records is $81,000. As in the past, we would expect interest on our borrowings to be at the best rate offered by XYZ Bank.

Presently, you are holding a note in the amount of $81,000, which is due on May 12, 19___. We expect to repay the note and accrued interest on that date, and will not be borrowing from you again for a month or two. However, we do anticipate utilizing the full line during most of the remainder of the year.

Your financial support and the many services of your bank are greatly appreciated.

Cordially,

ALTERNATE WORDING

The first paragraph, in this case indicating enclosure of the annual report of the company, is not conventional. However, it may be valuable for the company to establish its sound financial condition and to put it on record with the bank.

The second paragraph may start, depending upon the specific situation: "This will confirm our agreement concerning the extension of our line of credit to (date) . . ."

5. OPENING A SAFE DEPOSIT BOX

Opening a safe deposit box is not a matter of small import to a company. The box will hold valuable records, which, if they fall into the wrong hands, could do irreparable damage to the company. The authorization for access must be quite specific in all regards.

General Approach

Actions involving bank transactions such as this require the authorization of the board of directors. Therefore, the instrument by which the authorization is made should be stated. Since, in this case, a box is already open, changes in authorized personnel are noted. If this were an application for a new box, the names of all the authorized individuals would be listed within the letter or in an attachment. Such a list remains with the bank and is changed as each change is indicated by the company.

The use of two signatures on the letter follows the practice of the company in using two signatures on such documents. This is a matter of company practice, followed rather widely, but is not necessarily a requirement except as specifically determined by the company itself.

model letter A.5

Gentlemen:

On December 12, 19___ the Board of Directors of ABC & Co., Inc., adopted   **(a)**
a resolution authorizing certain officers of this Corporation to rent safe deposit
boxes in the name of the Corporation and also to name those individuals who
should have access to these boxes. You have a copy of this resolution
in your files.

In accordance with this resolution, this letter is your authority to make certain   **(b)**
changes in the list of persons having access to our safe deposit box at your
bank, effective immediately.

Mr. Joseph W. Mann, of our St. Louis office, is to be added to the list of persons
authorized to have access to our safe deposit box at your bank. Please forward
signature cards, for specimen of Mr. Mann's signature, directly to his attention
at our St. Louis office, 222 Main Street.

You will note that we are not changing the basis on which access is to be had   **(c)**
to our safe deposit box; that is, access only by any two of the people named
on the list.

Very truly yours,

ALTERNATE WORDING

This letter is too complete for most situations. If necessary, various portions
could be deleted if not applicable.

(a) Enclosed is a copy of a resolution adopted by the Board of Directors of
    Robert Greene & Co. authorizing certain specified corporate officers to rent
    safe deposit boxes in the name of the Corporation. In that resolution is a

listing of names and corresponding titles of individuals who are currently authorized to have access to such boxes.

(b) This letter is your authorization to send signature cards to each of the individuals listed in the resolution. Please send such cards directly to the individual named by registered, not certified or regular, mail.

(c) Please note that the basis for access, in accordance with the resolution, is by any two individuals on the list at any given time.

6. CLOSING A BANK ACCOUNT

Action to close a bank account requires the vote of the board of directors. This action, recorded in the minutes of the board meeting, constitutes a statement of authorization only; until the letter is written indicating the actual termination, no action will be taken by the bank to close the account. The signatures of two corporate officers are called for in this instance, as in most transactions involving banks.

General Approach

Indication of the action of the board and the fact that authorization exists has to be given. If the authorization had not been previously transmitted to the bank, it could be included as an attachment to this letter.

Because the account is to be closed, the funds have to be transferred. The second paragraph tells the bank how the transfer is to be made; in this case a check is to be drawn for the balance and mailed to the treasurer, who will probably deposit it in another account or another bank.

model letter A.6

Gentlemen:

In accordance with the terms of the resolution adopted by the Board of Directors of ABC & Co., Inc., at a meeting on June 26, 19___, certified copy of which you have on file, this letter serves as notice that ABC & Co., Inc., is terminating its account with the XYZ Bank of St. Louis.

Would you please see that a check covering the balance in this account is **(a)** mailed to us, at the above address, to the attention of the Treasurer, Mr. Edward Brown.

(b)

Very truly yours,

ALTERNATE WORDING

(a) We are terminating this account concomitant with the closing of our local office on (date). Please forward a check covering the balance in the account to our headquarters office, to the attention of the Treasurer, Mr. Edward Brown.

(b) Subsequent to the closing of the account, please forward all outstanding drafts to your Forest Lawn branch for payment. By this letter, we are notifying your Forest Lawn branch to honor the outstanding checks drawn on your branch.

7. OPENING A NEW BANK ACCOUNT

Businesses do have to open bank accounts, just as they have to close them; this is a fact of business. Various precautions have to be taken to assure the safety of funds by preventing unauthorized persons from access to the account. This is provided in the normal fashion by following the procedures established by the particular bank and by the laws that apply, both federal and state.

Opening an account involves some prior negotiation on the part of the bank and the company. It may be assumed that the selection of the bank by the company has been made after careful consideration of facilities and services, location, and other important factors.

General Approach

Opening an account involves either an action on the part of the board of directors or the authority of one or more corporate officers. If the latter is the case, the authority has to be cited and a copy of that authority transmitted to the bank, just as does a resolution of the board of directors.

If there are any special instructions, as there are here, for instance, they must be spelled out quite clearly and unambiguously. An unusual condition stated in this letter is that the bank is asked to transfer funds to another bank on a daily basis, meaning that there will likely be few withdrawals from this account. This leads to the situation where "bad checks" are likely. Virtually any withdrawal will cause an insufficiency of funds. In this instance, the company has agreed in advance that it will accept charges resulting from the action of the bank in following the instructions given.

The offer to answer questions is a matter of simple courtesy in most situations; here it becomes necessary because of the special conditions requested. The closing is conventional but friendly.

model letter A.7

Dear Mr.——————

Enclosed is a copy of (Company Name) standard Resolution of the Board of Directors, signed signature cards and our check for $100 opening an account with the Airport Branch of your Bank.

(Company Name) instructions for the treatment of this bank account are as follows: **(a)**

  1. Transfer of Funds

      Please transfer any funds, down to a $100 balance, daily, to our Account #——————— at the ——————— Bank in Phoenix for deposit to the credit of (Company Name) to the attention of Mr. ———————, Controller.

  2. Bad Checks

      We ask that any check that is returned "Insufficient Funds" automatically be entered for collection, advising the paying bank to hold for 10 days.

      We also ask that any check returned for another reason be charged back against our account and returned to the Station Manager.

      We further request that in the debit advice to our account you list the following on all chargebacks: The name of the drawer, the reason the check is returned and the amount.

      On all collection advices, please provide a copy of the advice with the bank statement and show the name, the gross amount and any service charge.

  3. Corrections

      We ask that you give us detailed instructions as to the reason for the correction; i.e., errors in addition, listing of checks, etc.

  4. Bank Statements

      We ask that monthly bank statements be on a calendar month basis and be mailed to ——————————— to the attention of Mr. ———————, Controller.

If you have any questions regarding the above, or if any further information is required, please do not hesitate to contact me.

We wish to thank you for your cooperation and look forward to a long and profitable relationship.

Very truly yours,

ALTERNATE WORDING

The detailed instructions given in the letter serve for a specific requirement. They may be used as applicable. For most purposes the following will serve as a general statement:

(a) We trust that all services of the bank will be made available to us and to our employees on the usual basis. We will appreciate your acknowledgment of this letter and the signature cards on the duplicate copy of this letter.

8. NEW POWER OF ATTORNEY

Determination of who shall have power of attorney rests with the board of directors. In such instances where powers of attorney are changed, the banks must be so advised.

General Approach

Authority to make changes is cited and, in this case, it is the action of the board of directors at a meeting of which minutes are on file at the bank. Pursuant to decisions made at that meeting, the change in the power of attorney can now be made.

The name or names of each of those persons who are no longer to have power of attorney are given. The name or names of the persons who shall be allowed power of attorney are also given. In this sample, the signature cards of the bank were provided in advance by the company; they need not be. As a result of having taken all action unilaterally, the letter and authorization now have to be acknowledged. Were the bank to have to send signature cards and indicate that they were for the named signatories, the return letter would constitute the acknowledgment.

The second letter, signed by two corporate officers, serves the same purpose as the first letter, except it is notification only, without signature cards requested, for the action. It should probably carry a request for an acknowledgment.

model letter A.8

Gentlemen:

We have previously furnished you a certified copy of resolutions adopted by the Board of Directors of ABC Industries, Inc., on April 27, 19___, authorizing certain officers of the Company and officials of its Divisions or Groups to revoke or add signatories to bank accounts maintained by the Company and its Divisions or Groups.

In accord with the provisions of the above-mentioned resolutions, the authority heretofore granted to J. J. Murphy and R. H. Parkhill to sign checks on Control Account No. 227 202-4, when payable to ABC CRANE, HOIST & TOWER DIVISION OF ABC INDUSTRIES, INC., is revoked, effective immediately, and P. J. Bettendorf is hereby designated a signatory on such account.

We are enclosing a signature card properly executed by Mr. Bettendorf.   **(a)**

We will appreciate your acknowledging receipt of this letter by signing the enclosed duplicate in the space provided and returning it to us.

Very truly yours,

ALTERNATE WORDING

(a) Please send us signature cards for Mr. Bettendorf.

model letter A.8A

Effective June 1, 19___, Peter Kande is no longer authorized to draw checks against ABC & CO., INC.'s, accounts with The XYZ Bank of St. Louis, St. Louis, Missouri.

Effective June 1, 19___, Edward J. Brown is hereby authorized as Treasurer of the Corporation to draw checks against ABC & CO., INC.'s, accounts with The XYZ Bank of St. Louis, St. Louis, Missouri.

Sincerely,

9. SUGGESTIONS FOR BANK SERVICES

Upon occasion, any official of a company that enjoys the respect of its community will be asked to contribute ideas or time to improve commercial services available to all industries in the area. This is such a letter, although its contents are of a specific nature, related to the questions raised at a meeting addressed by the author. It is an unusual occurrence when a speaker is not asked to formalize some of the points in a talk he gives, particularly if the talk is informal. A controller or treasurer should be prepared to follow up any talk with some brief written notes on his talk.

General Approach

Since a letter of thanks is socially obligatory for one who has been invited to speak before a group, the framework for the follow-up letter is established. The details will follow the outline of the talk, but stated, as shown, very briefly.

model letter A.9

Dear Mr._____:

Thanks again for your kind hospitality last night. I enjoyed meeting and talking with all of your group. It occurred to me this morning that you might find some use for the notes I had made for myself regarding possible actions or programs any bank might undertake. For whatever they are worth, these are the ideas I noted:

1. Counsel companies (particularly smaller ones) on advantages and methods of cash forecasting, both long and short term. Explain how they can best meet their needs. Advise on how to invest and in what instrument to meet their best interest.

2. Educate smaller banks on "prime rate," average vs. minimum balances for corporate customers, diversity of balances, reasonable service charges, etc.

3. Consider sponsoring forums of bankers and company financial officers— we have plenty of local talent.

4. Can bank develop a short-term mutual fund to accommodate small investors at higher yields than they can earn individually?

5. How many small companies really understand cost of borowing vs. cost of losing cash discounts? Also, inverse relationship of interest rate to cost of fixed type money market instruments?

6. Problems of small companies with delayed collections due to large customers working cash very hard.

7. Ultimately, if not sooner, competition will soak up excess balances if banks don't advise their customers. Good customers, who might otherwise be lost, may well be retained by bank which advises them honestly of necessary balances to support the activity or credit line and does not try to hold on to excess balances, except perhaps in form of CD's if yield is competitive.

Cordially,

10. REQUEST TO STOP PAYMENT OF CHECK

One value in the use of checks in the transaction of business is the relative safety and traceability of the material. Human error can be compensated for in the loss of a "draft" while it cannot, without much more effort, be overcome when dealing with cash. Also, checks are easily transported through the mails, and checks are not negotiable until made so, giving relative safety in that area. Unfortunately, the safety is limited to dealings of honest people, and the need to protect against illegal activities is still present. The purpose of stopping payment of checks is obvious: it is to avoid having an illegal draft of funds made by someone performing a criminal action or to avoid a draft of funds by someone or some company for a variety of legitimate reasons.

A request for "stop payment" is much like the request for the bank to honor the original draft for payment. It is authorized in the same manner and, if possible, by the same person who signed the check.

The acknowledgement from the bank is much in the form of their clearing statement, which appears on the back of each check. Seldom does a stop-payment order have to be renewed when the check has been made out to a company, since the practice of honoring only up to 90 days frequently involves verification by the bank with the maker if the check is still valid. On orders that affect individuals, such as stockholders, for instance, it may be necessary to keep the stop-payment order in force for years, since stockholders have been known to hold checks without cashing them for periods of up to several years.

General Approach

The request to stop payment must contain all the information contained in the original draft. These are: check number, date, amount, and payee. If the stop-payment order is made by someone other than the original signer, the name of the person who signed the check should also be indicated.

The reason for stopping payment may be supplied at the option of the maker. In this case, the reason involves a possibility of foul play and alerts the bank to anticipate a possible illegal claim. On the other hand, if the reason for stopping payment involves a dispute with the payee, it might be better if this matter were not made public. In a dispute, payment may be made after the dispute is settled. As sometimes occurs, the dispute is a result of misunderstandings, and to expose the payee to the maker's reasons for stopping payment may be patently unfair to the payee.

model letter A.10

Gentlemen:

Please place stop-payment order against our Check A 036187, dated December 11, 19___, payable to ABC Industries for $283.90.

We have been notified by the payee that their deposit of December 17, 19___   **(a)** was lost in transit to the bank and no trace found of it.

Sincerely,

ALTERNATE WORDING

(a) We have been notified by the payee that our check was not received by them. We are issuing a duplicate check to cover our payment to them. Should the original be presented for deposit by the payee, please notify us promptly.

11. CHANGE OF CORPORATION TREASURER

From time to time, changes in personnel take place at the level of controller and treasurer. At such times, it is necessary to inform all banks with which the company has dealings that such changes have taken place. It is also necessary to notify various other parties and certain governmental agencies, but these latter may be taken care of by the attorneys for the corporation.

Except where the outgoing treasurer or controller is leaving under "a cloud," it is reasonable for the outgoing official to notify the banks of his departure from his rather sensitive position. He could do it by means of the formal notice of the action of the board of directors in making or authorizing the change. Or, as this letter shows, he may, and as a matter of courtesy, probably should give his former business associates the warmth of a personal letter.

General Approach

Basic notice of this change is provided to the bank official, giving effective date of the change, usually some time in the future. It is likewise necessary to notify the bank to remove the old name from their records of persons authorized to sign for withdrawals from the accounts held by the bank.

Since many of the relationships between controllers and treasurers and bank officials become fairly close after years of association, it is fitting that the outgoing official thank his banker for courtesies extended to him in the past.

Formal notice of the change is needed to meet the requirements of the law in such matters, so it is either attached to the letter or transmitted separately. In this instance, it is an enclosure, probably the better means since instructions concerning its use are given in the letter.

Whether asked for or not, the signature cards would have to be sent for the new official to sign. Since many national companies maintain offices in more than one location and use banking facilities at each location, the address to which the signature cards are to be sent should be indicated. If, however, the company operates from only one location, this may be omitted. Still another possibility may arise: where the treasurer does not maintain an office at corporate headquarters, in which case his full address would be indicated.

model letter A.11

Dear Mr. Doe:

This is to advise you that Edward J. Brown has been elected Treasurer of ABC   **(a)** & Co., Inc., effective June 1, 19___, taking over that office which I have filled for the past 8 years. In view of this change, would you please add Mr. Brown's name to the list of persons authorized to draw checks against our Regular, Payroll and Petty Cash accounts with your bank. At this time, would you also remove my name from the list of authorized signers.

I want to express my appreciation for the service that your bank has given us in the past and I expect to have a continuing relationship with you in my position as Vice President of ABC & Co., Inc.

I am enclosing formal notice of this change, signed by Everett Miller and myself in accordance with the resolution passed by our Board of Directors on June 26, 19___, certified copy of which you have on file.

Would you please forward signature cards for specimen of Mr. Brown's signature directly to our offices in New York.

Very truly yours,

ALTERNATE WORDING

As appropriate, wording and tone should be changed to reflect authorship of the letter by the incoming treasurer, as for example:

(a) This is to advise you that I have been elected Treasurer of ABC & Co., Inc., effective June 1, 19—, taking over that office which was so ably filled for the past 8 years by Mr. Edward J. Brown. In view of this change, would you please add my name to the list of persons authorized to draw checks against our Regular, Payroll and Petty Cash accounts with your bank. Your authority for this action is contained in a copy of the official minutes of the Board of Directors (copy enclosed).

12. Notice to Bank of Special Authorization for Public Accountant

Special authorizations are needed for accounting and auditing purposes at various times during the year. Normally, some sort of pre-arrangement will be made with the bank to notify them that such arrangement is to be made. Because of the rather routine nature of such requests, a short written note for the record is all that is required.

General Approach

The letter will be addressed to the bank to the specific attention of a bank officer, generally a vice-president who handles the company account. It might be addressed as shown or addressed directly to the attention of the bank official himself.

The text of the letter is straightforward and routine. There are no special items. In this particular letter, the second sentence is a reference to a prior contact on this subject. If such contact has not taken place, omit this reference.

Since this is a formal communication, as written, the closing is formal. If the letter had been addressed to an individual, the closing could have been "Cordially," rather than "Yours very truly."

model letter A.12

Gentlemen:

This letter will serve as your authorization for submitting to ABC & Co., of 2 2nd Ave., New York City, the cutoff statement of our Special Account. This is in accordance with our telephone conversation yesterday afternoon and is a follow-up to the letter of December 29, 19___, which was signed by Mr. Louis Wolff.

(a)

Yours very truly,

Alternate Wording

A paragraph may be added here, as follows:

(a) As appropriate, authorized representatives of ABC & Co. will be in contact with you concerning specific items listed in the statement. Please extend to them the usual courtesies you have always given us.

group B

CREDIT SITUATIONS
INVOLVING CUSTOMERS

Credit Situations Involving Customers

Probably the most important and time-consuming function of a corporate controller or treasurer involves collection of monies due for products or services provided by his company. Even when a company employs a credit manager to conduct much of this type of correspondence, questions involving the extension of credit to customers will have to be resolved by the controller in all but routine situations. Certainly, the controller is accountable for all delinquencies and for assuring the eventual, if not the prompt, payment of all amounts due.

In addition, the controller is responsible for any special credit terms that are not considered routine. In the smaller company, he will be responsible for all negotiations involving credit extended or denied. He is expected to use good judgement in the granting of normal credit terms to new customers; in obtaining payment from former customers who previously had been good credit accounts and who have fallen in arrears, and to do this without antagonizing the account because they may again become more solvent; in dunning poor payers; and in extending credit to new companies that have no experience from which to judge.

These obligations put a serious strain on the controller. He must convey, forcefully at times, the urgency of having customers pay their bills. At the same time, he must try to avoid making implied or outright threats unless he is in such a position and desirous of following through. Use of form letters avoids the undesirable personal confrontation. Although the language may appear "stiff," it serves its purpose by making the request appear routine and not prompted by any particular action on the part of the customer.

It is not always possible for a company fiscal officer to learn the reasons for a customer's failure to meet his obligations. Insofar as possible, all letters relating to credit situations should presume, in the absence of any other indications, that the customer is dealing in good faith. Any other course could endanger a future profitable relationship and damage the goodwill of the controller's own company.

The following group of letters represents a consensus of approaches by several companies. In appearance, they have a surprising unity of approach, which makes one letter from one company almost a companion piece to another letter from another company. They all represent studied approaches and provide excellent samples for both the experienced controller and the inexperienced assistant credit manager.

1. Notification to Customer of Your Refusal to Sell to Him Because of His Poor Credit Rating

A key marginal note on the office copy of this letter provided the reasoning that led to the refusal of the credit manager to extend credit to this customer. The note read: "This is an account that we do not want unless we can secure reliable figures warranting our extending credit. Our D & B report shows that ABC & Co. and DEF Co. are one and the same."

The credit manager would rather forego the potential business than to have a bad debt on his hands. Nevertheless, even his internal note indicates a willingness to oblige the customer if favorable credit information could be obtained—although he seems to doubt that this would be possible.

General Approach

Because of the poor risk, the seller does not wish to extend any credit terms, even to accept cash, because he can foresee the possibility of having the customer refuse to accept the order, which has to be made up or cut to a given requirement. This would involve an expense to the seller not covered by the amount of the transaction, presuming, of course, that the sale is made at normal prices and under normal sales conditions, without penalties. Since it is not possible for the controller to predict what may occur, it is not feasible for him to ask for penalties in advance; even the avoidance of penalty-causing action could involve expense to the seller.

Refusal to sell to a customer because of his poor credit rating should not be coupled with implied promises. As this letter shows, the seller will oblige only when his conditions are met on a normal and routine basis.

Common courtesy indicates that the reason for rejection be given. Merely to say that you reject because of a "poor credit rating" is begging the question. Also, it is not only discourteous, but it may imply that you have possession of information that may be potentially damaging to the customer, information that may or may not be true. Recent legal decisions have held that an individual can collect damages when refused credit based upon hearsay. Although this may or may not apply to corporations, it is never a good practice to withhold the reason for refusal to grant credit.

model letter B.1

Gentlemen:

We acknowledge receipt of your order for 6 pieces of upholstery fabric but our **(a)**
source of trade information shows the latest financial information available
is your financial figures of 12-13-___ which showed current assets of $8,772,
current liabilities of $26,336, and deficit in your surplus account.

We will need a copy of your financial statement of December 31, 19___ showing **(b)**
a much improved position before we can ship on open account terms. We do
not ship C.O.D. or on cash in advance terms due to the special handling involved;
therefore we will appreciate your forwarding the desired information to us at
the earliest possible date.

Very truly yours,

ALTERNATE WORDING

(a) We acknowledge receipt of your order of recent date but information that
has come to our attention indicates that legal action is pending for collection
of monies owed by you to several creditors.

(b) Pending settlement of claims and liens against (name of company) we feel
that it would not be in our best interests to accept orders from you on
open account or special terms.

(b) When your credit position is improved, we would be pleased to reconsider
your request for credit. Until that time, however, we cannot accept your
orders.

2. REQUEST TO CUSTOMER TO PROVIDE ASSURANCES OF HIS FINANCIAL STABILITY DUE TO BANKRUPTCY PROCEEDINGS

Any company that must manufacture a product to order is extremely vulnerable when attempting to deal with a poor credit risk, and it is particularly vulnerable when bankruptcy has been declared by the customer and the customer is operating in receivership. To some degree, a company that ships off the shelf has a similar problem but stands to recover its merchandise in due time if payment has not been received and if the merchandise still exists. Nevertheless, all caution should be taken to avoid extending open credit terms to a bankrupt customer; his obligation to repay is significantly less than a company in more sound financial condition. Certainly, assurances should be received before entering an order under the conditions described.

In this particular type of situation, and in others like it, all suppliers will have been notified of the bankruptcy action, so it is possible for the suppliers to establish suitable actions. A marginal note on the internal copy of this letter read: "Payments of January show them past due and slow with all suppliers." Knowing this history, the controller, treasurer or credit manager will have to judge whether or not he even wishes to keep the door open to further negotiations.

model letter B.2

Gentlemen:

We acknowledge receipt of your order for upholstery fabric but the petition for arrangement under Chapter XI of the Bankruptcy Act, which you filed a petition for on March 3, 19___, prevents us from shipping on open account terms.

We will require a complete and current financial statement and profit and   **(a)**
loss statement bearing the signature of the president of your firm and the
certificate of your accountant before we can even consider entering your order
into our production schedule.

If you prefer, you may have your accountant fill out and certify the attached   **(b)**
form and return it to us. Upon receipt, we will be glad to notify you of the line
of credit available to your firm.

Very truly yours,

Alternate Wording

(a) We will ship the material upon receipt of payment in full or upon receipt of information that you have discounted the amount of the invoice.

(b) Until such time as we receive assurances of increased financial responsibility, we are ready and willing to continue to serve as a supplier on these special terms only.

3. REQUEST TO CUSTOMER FOR CREDIT INFORMATION

When a customer buys infrequently, it may be necessary to bring his credit information up to date. This does not imply that his credit is not good, but only indicates that it may be desirable to have current credit data in the event the customer places an order. This way, the order will not be held up pending receipt of updated credit information.

A request for up-to-date credit information may also serve as a reminder to the customer that he has not placed any orders lately. It is, in fact, a marketing letter to obtain new business, sent out in the guise of a credit letter. Since any company would rather have a good paying customer in its active accounts rather than in its inactive ones, this technique can be the controller's or treasurer's way of stimulating new business activity.

General Approach

This sample letter looks to the customer like a form letter, and it is, as it should appear to avoid inferring that his credit is not as good as it might be. Since the purpose of the letter is most likely not the seeking of credit data, the request for credit information should be almost perfunctory in tone.

model letter B.3

Gentlemen:

In reviewing your credit file, we find that we do not have a current financial statement and profit and loss summary on your company.

In order that we may bring your file up to date and better serve you with your   **(a)**
replacement parts requirements, please send us your latest balance sheet.
Naturally, this information will be kept in strict confidence and will be greatly
appreciated.

Thanks in advance for your cooperation.   **(b)**

Yours very truly,

ALTERNATE WORDING

(a) This, based on our present dealings, should be considered only as a formality that we observe to maintain our records in a current state. Naturally, this information will be kept in strict confidence.

(b) If there have been significant changes in your financial standing in the past year, especially on the favorable side, we would appreciate having you call special attention to them. Your assistance in helping us maintain our records is much appreciated.

4. GRANTING CREDIT TO A NEW CUSTOMER

In every business, there comes a time when credit has to be extended to a new customer. This is a most desirable situation, and controllers and treasurers hope that this will occur with greater frequency than it normally does. Every new customer gained—particularly one who pays his bills—provides an additional measure of secure business. Several possibilities can be involved concerning the granting of credit, each involving a different approach: first, when the seller seeks out the customer and offers him credit for that time in the future when he may wish to make a purchase (this is the manner in which department stores solicit credit accounts); second, when the buyer places an order and is granted credit for that order; third, when credit is requested by the buyer for his eventual use, although this is not very different from the foregoing situation, except that no order has been placed.

The second situation described is the more customary situation faced by commercial business and is shown in the sample letter. However, although the customer is granted credit, particularly since the seller has acknowledged receipt of an order and indicates his willingness to fill it, the seller is undertaking to manufacture a product and hold it for shipment until the required credit information is received. Were this a consumer account, credit would first be checked by the seller, with shipment made only after satisfactory proof of the customer's ability and willingness to pay for the merchandise he ordered.

General Approach

Since it may be assumed on a general basis that the company entering an order has a conventional business system of its own, that company's personnel will require reference to their own records for the most rapid handling of correspondence. Therefore, the "reference" noted appears immediately upon opening the letter. The first short paragraph, referring to the order and thanking the customer, is rather conventional. However, it is necessary to note that formal acceptance will be covered separately—if that is the policy of the seller—either using the customer's order acknowledgment portion of his purchase order or in a separate letter from the vendor.

The second paragraph contains the key information. It needs no special comment.

Paragraph three is the request for prompt action. Obviously, neither party wishes to hold up shipment; the buyer because he wants the material, the seller because he wishes to be paid as soon as possible after shipment.

The closing is conventional.

Insofar as the particular policy of the seller requires, the wording can be modified to cover the particular situation and conditions. In particular, the question of timing of receipt of the desired information should be firm, especially if shipment is "off the shelf" or if special fabrication is required of a standard item with a long manufacturing lead time.

model letter B.4

Gentlemen:

Reference: Your Order No.

Thank you very much for the referenced order. Our formal acceptance will be **(a)** covered in a separate communication.

According to our records, this is our first opportunity to supply you with our **(b)** products. We would, therefore, like to have you submit credit information to us for our consideration in the establishment of an account for you on our standard terms of "full payment, net 30 days." You may use the enclosed business report form or you may supply equal information using your own format. In any case, please include the complete names and mailing addresses of your bank and several trade references. This information will be maintained in strict confidence by us.

(c)

We urge you to submit this information promptly so there will not be any shipping delay when your order is ready.

Again, thank you for your order and if we can assist in any way, please let us know.

Sincerely,

ALTERNATE WORDING

(a) We are in receipt of your above order, which has been referred to our order editors for handling.

(b) This transaction raises a question of mutually satisfactory payment terms. It would be fine if you could furnish us with the name of your bank and three trade references with complete addresses in order that we may establish open account credit in your favor in this amount.

When the company offers discounts for prompt payment, it may be appropriate to add the following paragraph:

(c) It is our policy to offer discounts of 2% for payments received within 10 days of date of invoice. We adhere rigidly to this policy. If, for any reason, we receive a later payment with the discount taken, you may expect to find the discount rebilled for payment on a subsequent invoice. Discounts are not offered on special order items.

5. REFUSAL TO GRANT CREDIT TO A CUSTOMER

At times, it is simply not good business practice to extend credit to a customer whose record of payments is poor. At other times, it is possible to allow limited credit or credit to cover only specified conditions of sale.

General Approach

Since the initiation of this correspondence was with the company seeking credit, the respondent replies to this point. From there on, the story is one in which a review of experience is given and the decision indicated.

model letter B.5

Dear Mr. _____:

Thank you for your renewed interest in our company as a supplying source for your exhaust and shock requirements. Our representative has forwarded the necessary forms to the Credit Department, awaiting credit approval for open account terms.

A review of your file indicates that the account was consistently plagued by slowness during our last business relationship. At one point, the account balance was over _____ days past due for payment during early 19__.

Because of this poor payment history, and to remain consistent with good business practices, I cannot now approve the account for open terms. This decision is regretful, but the circumstances leave no other choice.

(a)

(b)

(c)

Again, thank you for the consideration given our company.

Sincerely yours,

ALTERNATE WORDING

(a) Because of your poor payment history, and to remain consistent with good business practices, I cannot now approve the account for open terms. However, we are willing to consider your application for cash transactions. If this arrangement is acceptable to you, please let me know.

(b) If, after a reasonable number of dealings, we feel that open account terms can be allowed, we will notify you of our favorable decision.

An additional paragraph may be added here, as appropriate, as follows:

(c) We are receptive to a drawing account not to exceed an amount equal to the orders received by us for your account. This may be, at your option, on a revolving basis, or you may set a maximum limit.

6. INQUIRIES INTO CUSTOMER'S CREDIT REFERENCES

Depending upon the circumstances, a letter requesting credit information from a reference given by the customer may call either for general information (letter A) or specific financial data (letter B). It is possible for a situation to develop in which credit information of the sort requested in letter B would not be supplied because it might indicate, to the reference at least, that he might be exposing an error in judgment, which he would prefer not to have generally known. On the other hand, he may be perfectly willing to help another fiscal officer avoid a serious mistake and would supply the necessary data.

General Approach

Letter A shows a typical, matter-of-fact approach that would provide the information desired. The inclusion of a postage-paid envelope is a nice way of indicating that you do not wish to impose on the goodwill and time of the other controller any more than is absolutely necessary to avoid making an error yourself.

Letter B makes the answers even easier to provide. Just filling in the spaces will provide sufficient information for the writer. However, it virtually eliminates the possibility of obtaining an opinion, an opinion which may, in the course of determining the advisability of granting credit, be instrumental in its effect upon the ultimate decision.

There are times when a marginal fiscal statement could be indecisive, but several opinions of one sort or another could swing the decision one way or the other. Since the granting of credit is based so much upon the judgment of the individuals rather than upon fiscal strength, opinions should be solicited whenever possible.

model letter B.6A

Gentlemen:

The above customer has referred us to you for information regarding his credit.   **(a)**

In order that we may intelligently consider the advisability of opening a credit   **(b)**
account, we would appreciate your giving us any information which might be
helpful to us. Any information submitted will be kept in strict confidence.

A stamped, self-addressed envelope is enclosed for your convenience in replying.

Thanks in advance for your cooperation.

Sincerely yours,

ALTERNATE WORDING

(a) We have been referred to you by ABC Company, 2 2nd Ave., N.Y., for
information as to their credit responsibility.

(b) Information as to the capital investment and financial position of their
business, together with your opinion of their principles, will be greatly
appreciated and treated as confidential.

For consideration of a new account from a partnership or a sole proprietorship, a
different approach may be taken, as follows:

(b) In order for us to evaluate the advisability of opening a credit account, we
would appreciate any information concerning the company and the personal
characters of the principals. All information submitted will be kept in
strict confidence.

model letter B.6B

Gentlemen:

The above firm has given us your name as a credit reference. Please complete
the form below with your credit experience.

We assure you that any information given will be held in strict confidence. A
stamped, self-addressed envelope is enclosed for your convenience in replying.

Sincerely,

How Long Sold _____ Terms of Sale _____

Highest Recent Credit _____ Last Sale _____

Now Owing _____ Amount Past Due _____

Manner of Payments _____

Remarks _____

_____

By:_____

_____

Title

7. Notifying Customer of Refusal to Extend Credit to Him Because of His Failure to Supply Credit Information

It is entirely possible for a customer to be in excellent financial condition but to be refused credit by a supplier because the supplier has no information concerning his credit. Under such circumstances, it becomes necessary for the seller to restrict his sales to the customer until or unless the customer provides the required data. It is customary to request the credit data, and unless there is some reason to believe, beforehand, that the credit information may be uncomplimentary, the customer should be given the option of providing the information in any way he deems appropriate.

General Approach

Reference to the order is courteous and conventional. Reference to prior dealings, if any, is appropriate because it indicates goodwill on the part of the seller if the seller has previously extended credit without having had sound information on which to base a decision for or against the granting of open credit terms. From there on, terms and conditions that will be applied to future sales, subject to receipt of credit data, are spelled out.

The request for credit information is couched in general terms. It is general practice to allow the customer to choose the method of submitting credit information in lieu of any information that may suggest that this procedure is not likely to produce the desired results. In most instances, the names of suppliers who have already conducted business with the new customer would be acceptable. Other methods of establishing credit are open to the customer. Given different circumstances, the specific method by which credit information is to be provided might be spelled out in detail.

model letter B.7

Gentlemen:

We are in receipt of the above order from PQR Manufacturing Company,   **(a)**
Denver, Colorado.

This is the second order we have received. The first one, #4467, has been   **(b)**
released on open terms, but we do not have enough credit information available
to establish open credit for future orders.

We would, therefore, appreciate receiving a recent balance sheet together
with names and street addresses of five suppliers, or, any other information
which might help us to establish open terms.

Thank you for your co-operation.

Very truly yours,

ALTERNATE WORDING

(a) We are in receipt of your order No. 4619, dated October 21, 19__, for one
     dozen ring-necked widgets.

(b) Inasmuch as this is the first order we have received from your company and
     we have had no previous dealings, we cannot release the order on open
     terms without adequate credit information. We would like sufficient credit
     information to establish open credit for future orders.

8. REFUSAL TO GRANT CUSTOMER CREDIT BUT AGREEING TO CASH SALE

It seems that the aroma of money makes the possibility of selling to a customer
more desirable than the prospect of having to wait for payment. Anyone not
recognizing this fact of business life subjects himself to the likelihood of performing
work for which payment may either be late or not forthcoming at all. So, in order
to avoid the possible loss of a sale, it is sometimes reasonable to agree to sales terms
involving either payment with placement of an order or payment upon delivery
on C.O.D. terms.

This situation arises only when a firm order is placed by a customer whose credit
is not acceptable. Refused special credit terms in advance of the order, the customer
may force the issue by sending in a firm order, taking his chances that the order

will be honored and trusting that some sort of acceptable terms will be worked out. This might very well be the action of a newly formed company. Rather than send a check to cover every order placed with every supplier, the company will accept the conditions of advance payment or payment C.O.D., but only if specifically requested to do so.

General Approach

Except for the special conditions, which are stated, this is a conventional letter, one that does not imply the inability of the customer to pay his obligations. Instead, it states that the supplier has only limited information available to him concerning the credit rating of the customer, so he cannot make a judgment concerning the extension of credit. If payment is asked along with the order, or at some time in advance of shipment, the usual discount terms that apply, if any, should be granted to the customer.

model letter B.8

Gentlemen:

Thank you for your order #6829, received recently. **(a)**

Based on the credit information we have available, it is not possible for me **(b)**
to approve open account terms for you at this time.

(c)

In order to establish a favorable payment record and give us a history upon **(d)**
which to base a future credit decision, would you be willing to accept future
shipments on a C.O.D. basis? Order #6829 would have to be shipped with
these terms.

May I hear from you regarding this suggestion? If you should require additional
assistance, please feel free to contact me.

Very truly yours,

ALTERNATE WORDING

(a) We acknowledge receipt of your recent order #OH-206 and we are most
appreciative of your interest in our products.

(b) We regret that we are unable to record your order on open account terms on the basis of information available to us.

A paragraph might be added here:

(c) Although your first shipment was appropriately paid, we have no real basis for extending additional credit.

(d) We have the items available in inventory. We will have to adapt them to meet the conditions of your purchase order. This comprises a special order and we are not inclined to put this quantity into our production schedule unless you are willing to make an advance payment of $3,690.18 ($3,784.80 less 2½ % discount of $94.62). We simply cannot afford to run this risk of having these items on hand with these special modifications, should something prevent your ordering out this order in its entirety.

9. EXTENDING SPECIAL TERMS OF SALE

In certain industries, every product manufactured is made to special order. Just as certain commercial terms of sale have become codified to the point that standard contracts can be purchased at any commercial stationer, so certain special terms of sale may be offered so that a seller may obtain an order. Frequently, the order goes to the company—or seller—who offers the best payment terms, not necessarily to the one who offers the best or even the cheapest product. Terms of payment are established by the salesman, following established company policy. Frequently, the first payment, under such conditions, is due before any work is commenced by the seller. Since special engineering may be required, parts and services ordered and contracted for, and other special arrangements made for the project, payment in advance of a portion of the total is not at all unusual.

Under conventional business conditions, payments of smaller amounts may be spread over three or six payments, each 30 days apart. Larger amounts may be spread over a much longer period and, in large construction projects, payments may spread over the life of the project—possibly several years—with some obligations not due until after completion of a "shakedown" period.

General Approach

The sample letter indicates that invoices have been sent, although it is not necessary that invoices be involved. This is a form letter with fill-ins; the same information could be presented in narrative form of general correspondence.

Terms of payment refer to the order. If special terms are made at the time of the sale, they should appear in the order. If they do not, a good deal of difficulty can result. Special terms are not subject to verbal understandings, but require documentation agreed upon by both parties, which becomes part of the contract.

model letter B.9

Re: Your Order
    Our Order

Gentlemen:

We enclose our Invoice Number _____ and _____ in the amounts   **(a)**
of $_____ and $_____ and bill of lading representing shipment of
our above order, bearing the following terms of payment.

(Enumerate per order)

Will you please send your remittance direct to P.O. Box _____   **(b)**
_____, as set forth in our invoices.

If any additional information is required regarding our invoice, will you   **(c)**
please contact the writer by return mail.

Very truly yours,

ALTERNATE WORDING

(a) We wish to confirm that the special terms of payment agreed to in the order
are as follows: (enumerate per order).

(a) We wish to confirm the special terms of payment for the order noted above.
I refer to our conversation of (date) and am confirming the terms as
follows: (enumerate)

(b) Please remit the amount of the first payment, due at this time, so that we
may start work on the project.

(c) Please indicate your acceptance of these terms by return mail. If you find
that the terms listed here do not meet with your understanding from our
conversation, please call me. If you agree, please confirm by return mail.

10. REFUSING TO EXTEND SPECIAL CREDIT TERMS

Rather than be placed in the position of paying invoices 90 days (or more) late,
many companies prefer to establish special credit terms by prior agreement. Or, it
may be inconvenient at the end of a fiscal period for a customer to have open invoices
that are overdue by more than a "normal" length of time required for processing. To

avoid this contingency, a customer might request early shipment of an order but ask to have billing to be received after the beginning of a new accounting period.

Whatever situation prevails at the customer's end, the supplier must make those judgments that affect him and consider the likelihood of encountering additional delays in payment beyond the "net" period. In some businesses, it is not at all unusual for payment for goods or services to subcontractors to be held open until the prime contractor has been paid, or for only partial payment to be made immediately upon delivery with the remainder to be paid upon payment of the complete amount by the prime contractor's customer. Such situation occurs in dealings with the U.S. Government, for instance.

General Approach

When special terms are requested, two options are open: The first is to refuse to extend the terms and to make shipments for orders with standard terms only. The second option is to hold the order until such time as the special terms become, by the passage of time, standard terms.

Refusal to accept orders under special credit terms should be clearly and unequivocally spelled out. If special terms had been given previously, it should be made clear that these were extended under exceptional conditions and are not normally granted.

model letter B.10

Gentlemen:

Thank you for your $280.00 order presently at our warehouse, requesting   **(a)**
July 1 billing.

In reviewing your file, I note that we have extended these special terms to you   **(b)**
as recently as April 1, and April 27, but we did so as an exception, and not
as standard terms.

Because these are special terms, usually associated with larger orders, and   **(c)**
because you have frequently requested these terms, I cannot now approve
July 1 billing for this order. Accordingly, the order will be shipped with regular
terms, and be payable in July.

If extraordinary circumstances make our regular terms inappropriate, please
feel free to contact me for approval of special terms.

Thank you for your cooperation.   **(d)**

Sincerely yours,

ALTERNATE WORDING

(a) Thank you for your recent order received at our warehouse today.

(b) Unfortunately, we cannot honor your request for first-of-the-month billing with shipments being made presently. The only way we can insure first-of-the-month billing is to hold up the order and ship after the 25th of April.

(c) Accordingly, our warehouse will process your order and ship after the 25th of April. This will allow you the requested terms. If you require shipment before this date, please notify our warehouse or me, and we will process the order immediately under our regular credit terms.

(d) I hope the above procedure does not cause you any inconvenience.

11. GRANTING CUSTOMER CREDIT UNDER SPECIAL CONDITIONS

Every company wishes to do as much business as possible and to do that type of business which shows promise of yielding an eventual profit. To assure itself the business that is available, it will frequently have to extend credit to a customer who has shown in the past something less than exemplary action in payment of invoices. Nevertheless, in allowing for these fiscal "lapses," most companies would rather obtain the business that is obtainable than to lose the potential that could develop as a customer becomes increasingly more solvent or as the customer grows in size and orders in larger quantities.

General Approach

As indicated, a brief introduction expressing thanks for interest is in order. Also in order is the statement that credit is to be extended.

The critical paragraph is the one that indicates that certain limitations are to be placed upon the account, giving the reasons for imposing these limitations. In one case, the reason was an earlier bad experience with this particular customer. Alternately, it might have been a letter to a new customer whose references had not proved satisfactory.

In the final paragraph, the writer indicates the terms and conditions he has imposed. His closing is conventional.

model letter B.11

Gentlemen:

Thank you for your interest in our company as the supplying source for your requirements.

After reviewing your financial statement and the other information we were able to gather, we have approved a line of credit for you.

In reviewing your credit file, I note that our previous experience with you was **(a)** hampered considerably by slow trade payments. This is a situation that we don't want to recur.

It is with this understanding that we are now requiring you to discount your purchases with us, as a condition of credit extension. If we subsequently find that you are not discounting your open account purchases with us, we will be forced to discontinue service to you from our warehouse.

I trust that these arrangements will meet with your approval. Thank you for your cooperation.

Very truly yours,

ALTERNATE WORDING

(a) Although the information indicated an ability to meet your commitments, we have been informed that payments are normally quite late, running from 80 to 180 days past due. Also, on occasion, discounts for early payment have been taken by your company on such late payments.

12. REQUEST TO A NEWLY FORMED COMPANY TO PROVIDE ASSURANCES OF FINANCIAL STABILITY

Sooner or later every seller will have to deal with a newly formed corporation, or even with an individual customer who is not known to him. No credit rating will have been established because no credit ever existed.

This is hopefully the beginning of a long and mutually profitable relationship. In order to get it off on the right foot, suitable credit references must be given. In this letter, references are requested since it is obviously not possible to establish any payment history with any other suppliers. It is perfectly proper to refuse to deal with a new company until they provide suitable and acceptable credit references. Nevertheless, even these references provide no more than an indication of the esteem in which the principals of the new company are held by their bankers, friends, and others who may have previously done business with them in prior corporate associations or as individuals.

model letter B.12

Attention: Harold M. Flynn
          Treasurer

Gentlemen:

We acknowledge, with thanks, receipt of your Order No. 5254 covering various sizes of Hose Clamps, which clamps have a total value of $762.

Credit references to date indicate that you are a new business which started on **(a)** August 1, 19___. Due to the newness of your organization, we are unable to verify credit references and would, therefore, appreciate receiving your opening balance sheet as a means of determining open credit terms for the above-mentioned order.

(b)

Your consideration of the above will be appreciated.

Very truly yours,

ALTERNATE WORDING

(a) We would, therefore, appreciate having the names of the banks in which you have accounts, and any other data you may be able to supply as a means of determining the amount of credit we can extend to you.

(a) Because of our lack of experience with your company, we request a cash deposit equal to one half the amount of each order until we have established a firm record of mutually satisfactory dealings. Upon receipt of a check for $381.00, we will ship you your Order No. 5254.

As desired, a paragraph may be added here, as follows:

(b) Conditions of sale are noted on our order acknowledgments, while we state our terms of payment on our invoices. For prompt payment, we offer cash discounts.

13. GENERAL COLLECTION LETTER TO A POOR CUSTOMER

Consumer credit comprises as much of a problem as does commercial credit. Most companies find that they have to establish a set of collection letters, possibly as many as eight or ten in a series, timed for sequential distribution in an order designed to allow the customer sufficient time to pay past due accounts before court action is taken or a collection agent is employed. The cost of legal action or collection services is normally far greater than the cost of money involved in the loss of the use of the capital tied up in delinquent accounts.

The sample letter shown here would be one type used after a customer has proved both his incapability and unwillingness to pay for his purchases. Before his account has reached this point, he will have indicated any willingness to repay if he were truly unable to pay and would have come to some accommodation with his creditors.

General Approach

Every effort to avoid actions involving third parties; i.e., courts, collection agents, lawyers and others, is indicated. However, the threat is made that an action will be necessary, although not committed, should no attempt be made to remedy the situation. Whether the delinquent is an individual or a company, unfavorable publicity is the result of any legal action, and the writer can stress that inevitability so that the customer is aware of it. Unfavorable publicity for a company can result in similar actions by other creditors who may fear that they will lose their money if liens are not taken, possibly forcing the debtor company into bankruptcy. In the case of an individual, no blanket statements could be made, each person acting in his own way.

The "carrot" of a settlement has to be held out, whether in a single letter or in a series of letters. If the delinquent customer does accept the offer of settlement, under whatever terms may be allowed, the controller will have achieved his objective.

model letter B.13

Dear Sir:

Due to the very serious situation regarding your account, I am writing you **(a)** in the hope of avoiding court action.

If we are forced to have our attorney sue for the balance in addition to court costs, the judgment we will obtain will be strictly enforced as provided by the laws of the state.

Won't you cooperate with us in avoiding the publicity and embarrassment of **(b)** a court appearance? You can avoid this by mailing a payment of $_____ today. At the same time, arrangements must be made to pay the balance. I can help you in arranging a payment plan which you can maintain regularly and which will be fair to you and (name of Creditor). However, you must come in or phone me in order that we can discuss this plan.

(c)

Very truly yours,

ALTERNATE WORDING

(a) At the present time, our records indicate that you have not taken any action to clear up your account with us. It is our desire, and we are sure it is yours too, to settle this matter quickly and without unnecessary fuss.

(b) Won't you cooperate with us to settle this matter? A start toward settlement is all we ask at this time and an indication on your part of willingness to close the account.

If the customer has been inordinately delinquent, a suggestion of how he (or she) may take the first step toward settlement may be added, as follows:

(c) If you will mail a payment of $100.00, which represents only a portion of your outstanding balance, we will both be able to avoid a situation which might prove embarrassing to you. At the same time, arrangements must be made to pay the balance.

The remainder of the paragraph to the closing can be the same as the last sentence in paragraph (b) of the sample letter.

14. GENERAL COLLECTION LETTER TO A GOOD CUSTOMER

Collections require a large part of a controller's time and effort. He alone is responsible for obtaining payment once his company has accepted an order and made shipment, just as it was his responsibility to approve the credit of the customer in advance of acceptance of the order. Sometimes, inexplicably and unavoidably, a good customer will fall in arrears in payment of a number of invoices. (A poor customer would never be allowed to have more than one or two open orders.) In order to avoid embarrassing or antagonizing the customer, the notice of past due invoices is most suitably presented in the style of a form letter.

General Approach

Using a form letter, such as letter A, the open invoices are listed. No comment concerning willingness to pay or ability to pay is made. Every consideration is given to the customer.

In the follow-up form B, the same approach is used, but the language is changed to reflect the fact that this is a second request. The use of a second request presumes that the customer failed to provide any suitable response to the first request. Nevertheless, the customer is still given the benefit of any doubt. One change is made indicating that payment in response to the letter is not now expected, as it was with the first notice. So, a request is made for notification of when payment may be forthcoming. Of course, should this notice go unheeded, the standing of the customer is liable to change. We may reasonably asume that payment of invoices listed in the first notice is overdue by more than a normal 30-day period. Given time for transmittal, action and receipt of payment, the second notice would not likely be sent sooner than two weeks later, and more likely the following month, making the payments now overdue by 60 days or more.

model letter B.14A

Attention: Accounts Payable Supervisor

Gentlemen:

We show that the following invoice(s) have not been paid:

DATE	NUMBER	AMOUNT
_____	_____	_____
_____	_____	_____
_____	_____	_____
_____	_____	_____

For your reference, we are enclosing a copy of our invoice(s). We would appreciate your remittance. If there is some reason why payment cannot be made, please advise us.

Very truly yours,

model letter B.14B

Att'n: Accounts Payable Supervisor
SECOND REQUEST

Gentlemen:

On _____ 19___, we forwarded you a copy of the following invoice(s) and a request for payment:

DATE	NUMBER	AMOUNT
_____	_____	_____
_____	_____	_____
_____	_____	_____

As of today, we have not received your check and, therefore, we ask you to please advise us when payment will be forwarded. An early reply will be greatly appreciated.

Very truly yours,

15. SERIES OF COLLECTION LETTERS ACCORDING TO AGE OF ACCOUNT—LONG SERIES

One of the most unrewarding tasks for a controller or treasurer is to try to collect past due accounts. Dunning letters are almost never sent out in less than 60 days after the normal time for net payments. Normal time may be 30 days, based on current commercial practice. That means that the customer has already had 90 days in which to pay. If, as has occurred several times in the past 20 years, money becomes extremely tight, good judgment demands that additional time be extended before collection letters are sent.

The set of letters that follows could represent a period of eight months, following the practice of sending one letter each month. This means that legal or other action would not be taken for a year after the delinquency commenced. Certainly, this is a very reasonable time allotment. If circumstances require, the time period for the series could be shortened, with one letter going into the mails every ten days or every two weeks. If allowance is made for normal mail delivery, processing time and return of mail, no less than ten days should elapse between letters. At its shortest, this still represents a time period of six months of arrears.

General Approach

Each letter contains either a threat of action or indicates an action already taken. Little by little, the customer is cut off from a supply, and little by little he is made aware of the direction in which the letters are pointing. Moving from a general request for action, the letters call for specific steps to be taken by specific dates, yet at no time does the writer seem impertinent and demanding.

The last letter in the series is sent by Certified Mail, Return Receipt Requested. Following this letter by ten days, a telegram is sent as follows:

"Important—No answer to our letter of (last date)."

This closes the door to further negotiation and the matter is given over to collection.

model letter B.15A

Gentlemen:

Our records show the following amounts outstanding on your account:

60 Days Past Due	$463.82
30 Days Past Due	(32.61)
Current	(13.55)
Total Account Balance	$417.66

Please send us your check to cover the above. If payment has already been mailed, please disregard this letter.

Sincerely,

model letter B.15B

Dear_____:

Your account is past due as follows:

DAYS	AMOUNT
30	$ 500.00
60	200.00
90	400.00
120	400.00
	$1,500.00

Unless a payment is mailed promptly it will be necessary for us to hold future orders.

So that we may continue to service your needs, please be sure your check is sent by return mail.

Sincerely,

model letter B.15c

Dear_____:

Your account is considerably past due. Because of this, we now have to temporarily discontinue open account privileges.

I regret having to impose this limitation, but your lack of response to earlier requests has left no other alternative.

May I please have your prompt cooperation with this matter so we can resume meeting your inventory requirements.

Sincerely,

model letter B.15d

Dear_____:

There is a balance outstanding on your account of $_____ of which $_____ is past due.

In order that we may continue to serve you from our warehouses and not place a restriction on your account be sure a check is sent by return mail.

It is important that this check be in our hands by _____.

Thank you in advance for your cooperation.

Sincerely,

model letter B.15e

Dear_____:

Because your account is considerably past due we have notified our warehouses to place a restriction on your account.

In order that we may open your account as quickly as possible, please be sure your check is sent by return mail for $_____.

It is important that we receive your check by _____.

Thank you in advance for your prompt cooperation.

Sincerely,

model letter B.15F

Dear_____:

We have outstanding and past due amounts which total $_____. We have attempted to work with you in resolving these delinquent balances, but you have failed to give us the courtesy of your cooperation.

We are now faced with placing your account with our attorney for collection. In good faith, however, we will defer making such a move for the next 15 days.

This period of time will allow you ample time to resolve this obligation and preserve your credit reputation.

Sincerely,

model letter B.15G

This letter is to be sent:

CERTIFIED MAIL, RETURN RECEIPT REQUESTED

Dear_____:

Prompt action is urged for the reason that within the next 10 days we shall have to forward a list of delinquent accounts to our collection agency and we are not anxious to have your name appear on it.

The past due balance on your account is $_____.

Will you forward a remittance or write us by return mail to avoid this drastic action.

Sincerely,

Telegram to be sent at the end of ten days:

Important—No answer to our letter of _____.

16. Series of Collection Letters According to Age of Account—Short Series

A distinguishing difference between a long collection series and a short collection series is the type of account involved. A long series is more appropriate when an individual, purchasing for himself, is concerned. A short series is more appropriate when dealing with an incorporated business or a company of some stature, whether or not incorporated. The long series allows the customer time to accumulate funds from income. The short series presumes that the customer has funds available to him or has the capability to obtain credit from appropriate financial institutions.

General Approach

In this particular set, the standard payment terms are Net 30 Days. This is conventional. After 30 days have passed since confirmation of receipt of the product or services, the first notice goes out automatically. It is merely a confirmation of the agreement and a notice that payment is now due.

Half a month later the second letter goes out. The elapsed 15 days should enable a delinquent account to make payment and for the payment to have been received. This letter is couched in stronger language but opens the door to the possibility that the customer is deliberately witholding payment because of lack of satisfaction. It does not allow for, nor should it, the possibility that the customer was unaware of his obligation, either through fault of the vendor or even failure of the mailed notice to reach the customer.

As so often can occur in large companies, the dissatisfaction of the customer is known by the sales department, but the sales department—because it is trying to satisfy the customer—does not convey notice of the problem to the accounting department. This second letter allows for this lapse but places responsibility upon the customer to make this situation known to the accounting department. It also very nicely presumes that the customer does not have the means to type out an envelope, or, more reasonably, that the customer might have missent his payment and needs a correctly addressed envelope.

The third letter, sent out either 15 days later or, depending upon the judgment of the Controller, still later, contains threat of collection. It gives a definite date by which payment must be received. This date, in effect, extends the deadline still further.

model letter B.16A

Re: Your Order
    Our Order

Gentlemen:

We are enclosing our Invoice Number _____ in the amount of $_____ and bill of lading representing shipment of our above order, bearing Net Thirty Days terms of payment.

In making payment of this invoice, please forward your check direct to P. O. Box _____, as set forth in our invoice.

Very truly yours,

model letter B.16B

Gentlemen:

We note on your attached statement charges prior to the current payment period of 45 days on Net Thirty Day accounts. We must request immediate payment of the past due items.

If for any reason the charge as shown is not due and payable, please give us details that will enable us to clear the item from your account.

We enclose a postpaid envelope for the immediate return of your check and/or reply direct to the writer's attention.

Very truly yours,

model letter B.16c

Re: Invoice No.
　　Invoice Date
　　Balance Due

Gentlemen:

This will be the last request which we will make direct to you on the unpaid invoices listed above.

If no payment has been received by March 31st, we shall take whatever steps are necesary to execute for collection.

Very truly yours,

17. COLLECTION LETTER WITH A LIGHT TOUCH

Anyone who receives a collection letter is probably more than a little annoyed when the first notice comes in with something on the order of: "We know that you will honor your obligation incurred by your purchase," or some such other almost insulting language. A first letter may be sent because the original notice of payment was lost in the mail, accidentally discarded with mail of no interest, or for any other reason. Certainly, a letter that imputes an attempt to avoid obligations honorably incurred will not get the best emotional response. Yes, it will obtain payment, since the customer never intended to withold his payment. But it also loses customers who feel that a dunning letter is not an appropriate first notice.

The approach taken in this sample, as can be seen, involves the fourth notice, not the first, yet it is still not a dunning letter. It is definitely a form letter, yet every once in awhile a form collection letter can be sent out that combines both the requirements of the message along with a lighter approach. Of course, these are only for those occasions when the use of a "light" approach does not compromise the message, or when the amount of money involved is not very large. Nevertheless, the appearance of a letter that appeals to the emotion rather than the intellect will gain an unusually high degree of attention, particularly in a business office. Very likely, if such a letter is received in a business office, the letter will "go the rounds" before it arrives for collection, particularly if the mail is opened in a mail room. It will become a source of embarrassment to the defaulting company.

Of particular value is the use of a letter embodying humor when the collection letter goes to an individual, such as the sample here. The amount of money is not large—in this case, probably not more than $5. The good-natured rather than the usually "sour" collection letter probably has more value than the usual type of letter that reaches customers every day.

General Approach

The pictorial approach used by *Better Homes and Gardens* * is light, but quite to the point. There is little verbiage and no attempt to be "cute." By keeping the wording to a minimum, the effect of the message is kept at a maximum. The reader is given a choice—all the possible choices considered for him by the writer of the letter, or all the choices that the writer wishes to allow. Unstated and unimplied is the threat of legal action. Nevertheless, this is an option that the recipient can choose for himself, should he wish to.

Recommendations for use of this type of letter include, as indicated, magazine subscriptions. It could be used in a wide variety of applications for collection, such as: spare-parts orders that have a minimum service charge of $10, $15 or even $25; charges for service calls on equipment on which the warranty has lapsed, but where charges are not of sufficient financial magnitude to jeopardize future sales; customers who are known to be having some difficulty temporarily in meeting financial obligations but whose previous credit has been excellent, etc.

18. Apology to Customer for Inability to Verify His Audit Statement

If in doubt, blame the computer. There are several letters in this collection in which the computer is responsible for whatever lapses have occurred. All too often that is the case, and it appears likely to be so for some years to come. Whether true or not, basing an apology on the computer is good business, even to the point of apology for late payment of invoices—accidental or deliberate. This can be overdone and should not be used too frequently, but, as this letter shows, the degree of inconvenience to the customer should be kept to a minimum. The computer cannot be blamed for slipshod bookkeeping practices, because that is an activity that can be monitored carefully by manual means.

Occasionally, a customer will request information concerning invoiced items that he questions. He may be questioning them because he has so many open orders with his suppliers that he needs assurance as to which invoices are due and which are not due. Or, at the end of an accounting period, his auditors will request verification of various items that they feel bear checking in the customer's accounts. This is conventional practice, and no harm would result if the information were not forthcoming for every item questioned.

The difficulty arises because the inability to supply information is a source of embarrassment to the seller. There is a possibility that the effect of this lapse might cause damage to the standing of the seller by indicating slipshod accounting practices.

---

* Reprinted with permission of the Meredith Corporation, Des Moines, Iowa.

model letter B.17

Dear Subscriber:

We're puzzled that we haven't received your check for the BETTER HOMES AND GARDENS subscription you ordered (this is the fourth letter we've sent you about it). May we at least get a pencil check from you in one of the squares below?

☐ Here is your check in full --
Thank you for your patience.

☐ Here's your money -- now leave me alone.

☐ Can't possibly make it today --
Will send one shortly.

☑ I mailed one yesterday.

☐ I don't intend to pay;
You'll have to fight for it.

That isn't too much to ask, is it, and as a further convenience, I'm enclosing a reply envelope. Please be sure to return the invoice with your payment.

He therefore must protect himself from implications of poor accounting procedures. This letter indicates that the seller is embarrassed, and it gives his reasons.

General Approach

This letter takes the form of an acknowledgment, explanation, apology and promise for prompt action in the future. For the record, it might be noted that "automated" does not necessarily mean "computer"; it could mean accounting or billing machine just as easily. It is a very useful catch-all term.

model letter B.18

Re: A/R Account No.

Gentlemen:

Thank you for your request for further information concerning your account with our firm.

Our recent conversion to an automated Accounts Receivable system has placed   **(a)**
us somewhat behind in our customer correspondence.

However, be assured that the questioned items on your account will receive our attention as quickly as possible.

Very truly yours,

ALTERNATE WORDING

(a) Our periodic audit, involving review of our records and confirmations of outstanding balances, delayed us in responding to our customer correspondence.

19. DELINQUENCY IN PAYMENTS DUE FROM SUBCONTRACTOR WHO RENTS SERVICES OR FACILITIES

Almost every large company, and many smaller ones, have facilities that are rented out, leased or otherwise subcontracted, for which payment is required. Companies have real estate subsidiaries that own the buildings in which manufacturing, administration, sales and other functions are performed. In the case of companies involved in transportation, leases are quite common for terminals and services, and companies with computers find excess capacity a valuable source of additional income. Such is the case in this letter, although it could apply equally well to a newsstand lease in the lobby of an office building, a vending machine operation in a company cafeteria or any other similar leasing arrangement.

When a delinquency in payments arises, either the delinquent is expected to make good shortly or the company will be obligated to terminate the arrangement and seek another lessee. This is not always easy and, rather than terminate a lease that has been mutually beneficial, some time may be allowed to lapse or an arrangement for interest can be made to cover a reasonable amount of delay in payments.

As can be seen, the delinquency has not approached the point where termination seems the only solution unless the lessee is able to make his future payments on time.

General Approach

It is absolutely necessary to inform the delinquent in writing that he is obligated to make his payments on time or else suffer the penalties agreed upon in the contract, and to have him acknowledge that he understands the situation and agrees that the steps to be taken are known to him and were previously known to him.

Since the delinquencies already incurred involve one month "slippage," the writer has cited the agreement and the amount of time that has slipped. He also indicates that, since the leasing agreement has different payments each month, the amount of the delinquency charge will be in proportion to the amount of the delinquency. In another type of situation, this portion of the letter would be changed appropriately.

As frequently happens, the leasing agreement is not the only one between the two companies and it is separate from other agreements for services or facilities. This is identified in the third paragraph.

In the fourth paragraph, the writer indicates the purpose of his writing. He has already cited the circumstances that prevail before he indicates the action he plans to take. This is particularly appropriate since his action is likely to be an unfavorable one.

The request for acknowledgment is essential and provides a suitable closing. The acknowledgment is requested on the letter itself to assure no possibility of misunderstanding.

model letter B.19

Dear Mr._____

This is to inform you that since May 12th, _____ Corporation has **(a)** been in violation of the delinquency settlement agreed to by our companies as of February 3, 19___. Per our mutual agreement, we have let the delinquency payments slide one month, providing the delinquency charge (1% interest per month) is paid currently. Based on this slide of one month, delinquency payments should be made as follows:

Date Due in My Office	Amount	Delinquency Charge	Total
Jun. 10, 19___	$12,000.00	$212.73	$12,212.73
Jul. 12, 19___	6,000.00	92.73	6,092.73
Aug. 10, 19___	3,273.31	32.73	3,306.04
Total	$21,273.31	$338.19	$21,611.50

These amounts are in addition to current invoices and must be identified as **(b)** such. As per the agreement dated February 3rd, the delinquency charge is assessed on the basis of 1% per month on the unpaid balance.

Should future delinquencies develop at any time, it is understood and agreed **(c)** that all (Company Name) computer and communications service to you will be terminated within twenty-four (24) hours.

Please acknowledge with your signature and date and return one copy to me.

Very truly yours,

_____

Controller

_____

Acknowledgment

_____

Date

ALTERNATE WORDING

(a) This is to inform you that your company is in arrears in the payment of rents, as per our contract of (date) by more than 30 days. As called for by the contract, this allows us to give you notice of eviction, which is our option to exercise upon due notice.

(b) We feel that this situation, having not occurred in the past, represents an oversight on your part or is of a temporary nature. Therefore, we have not elected to take action at this time.

(c) If there has been an emergency of the sort that has prevented you from making prompt remittance of your obligation, we would be pleased to work with you in a manner that would ease your financial load at the present time.

However, we ask that you let us know if such is the case; otherwise we have to assume that your delinquency results from some other cause.

(c) Should you fall further in arrears, or upon clearing this matter fall again in arrears, we reserve the right, under the contract, to exercise our option of cancelling the rental contract, with this letter serving as such notice of cancellation.

group C

SHAREHOLDER RELATIONS

Shareholder Relations

Despite the responsibility of the president in dealing with shareholders, his role is largely a ceremonial one. Most of the actual letter writing is performed by the treasurer or controller and is sent out over the signature of the president. In practice, shareholder relations are fiscal relations and fall completely within the purview of the fiscal officer of the company. He is responsible for assuring the verification of proxies for the annual shareholder meeting and for actually obtaining the proxies, even to the extent of having a second letter sent out to guarantee the required number of proxies for a legal meeting.

The fiscal officer is also the person who has to answer questions raised by shareholders concerning the management of various monies. There are many letters that cannot be shown in a letter book because they are so specific in nature that the likelihood of two such letters being written in even ten years by the same controller is extremely remote. In fact, some of these types of letters might be characterized as responses to "crank" types of letters. There is truly no way to anticipate the type of letter to which a suitable response can be given. The fiscal officer cannot possibly delegate this letter-writing task to his secretary by using a sample to follow, there being no precedent for a letter of this sort.

1. WELCOME TO A NEW SHAREHOLDER

When a person purchases a share in a company, he makes a personal commitment to the company. In a manner of speaking, he has "joined" his interest to the interest of the company: he has, in reality, become a part owner of the company. He may take his interest so seriously that he puts questions to the controller or treasurer concerning actions and accounting procedures of the company, and he is very likely to demand that certain correspondence come from the office of the president, since he would most prefer to have the president responsible to him as a shareholder.

Whether the matter is of sufficient importance to be answered by the president or whether it is of such a technical or routine nature that it would be handled in the accounting department, the name of the president is very likely to appear on the letter. Such is the case with notices of a general nature to shareholders concerning meetings, special news and other information. However, because of the special nature of this type of correspondence, the controller or treasurer is normally the person who actually writes the letters. It is with this situation in mind that some of the letters presented here may be expected to duplicate similar letters written by the president.

General Approach

A letter of welcome to a new shareholder is precisely and simply that: a letter of welcome. The president indicates his pleasure at learning the news that he has a new "owner." We may choose to believe that most purchases of stock are the result of the shareholder's interest in the company. If stock is not bought for speculation, the stock will be held for a reasonable period of time. Sending a report, whether the annual report or the most recent quarterly report, is a nice touch to "involve" the shareholder.

model letter C.1

Dear_____:

I have been advised by the company's transfer agent that you recently became   **(a)**
a registered holder of our common stock. I want to extend a most cordial welcome
into our family of shareholders and trust that your association with us will
be both pleasant and lengthy.

Our Annual Report for the year ended December 31, 19___ is enclosed herewith   **(b)**
because I know that same will be of interest to you.

If you should move to a new address, kindly send your new address as soon
as possible to our stock transfer agent, XYZ Trust Company of New York (Stock
Transfer Department), 2 2nd Ave., New York, New York. In providing this

information, please give your old as well as your new address and mention that you are a stockholder.

Sincerely yours,

ALTERNATE WORDING

(a) I would like to extend my personal welcome to you as a new shareholder in our company. I hope that your association with us will be both pleasant and lengthy.

(b) From time to time you will receive reports of activities of the company. These will include quarterly financial reports and copies of our company magazine, which are sent periodically to all our employees as well as to our shareholders.

2. NOTICE OF SHAREHOLDER MEETING

Regulations of the Securities and Exchange Commission make it quite clear that time limitations exist in the mailings of reports and proxy statements and notification of the annual meeting. Since these regulations are a matter of record and possibly subject to change, they need not be enumerated here. However, to cope with the requirements of the regulations, it is general practice—and most likely preferable— for the annual report and proxy statement to be mailed together along with notice of the annual meeting at which the proxy may be voted in person or mailed in to be counted.

Although the notice of the annual meeting is a form letter, it has to be composed each year to cover the various new conditions that are to be covered at the meeting. Since most shareholders have no intention of attending the meeting—nor could any large percentage ever hope to be reasonably accommodated by even a moderate-sized company—the letter and the request to return the proxy are probably the most important elements of the mailing to the shareholders.

General Approach

Every letter, even including this printed form letter, must bear a date. The salutation is definitive enough for the purpose.

The opening alerts the recipient to the inclusion of those documents that are legally required. Following this is the invitation to attend the annual meeting.

Because the company wishes to keep its shareholders informed—on the theory that an informed ownership is a more satisfied ownership, and shareholders are owners—the topics to be voted upon are listed. These are the same topics indicated in the proxy and in the proxy statement. Iteration is still appropriate in the letter since it is likely that many shareholders will go no further than the letter in their reading of the mail and then will mark their proxies.

A request to send in the proxy is made. A nice touch is added to remind the owners that if they fail to send in their votes, they will have to suffer the expense of another election.

Because so few people wish to attend annual meetings, the idea of having a card of admission serves to provide the management with information as to the number of people to expect—particularly if they plan to serve luncheon. It also serves, although this may not be possible, to exclude some persons who might wish to disrupt the meeting, as has happened so frequently in recent years.

Only the board of directors can speak for the owners, so the letter is signed by the senior operating officer of the corporation. Although the signature is that of the board chairman or president, the letter is normally composed by the controller or treasurer and given to the chief operating officer for his approval and formal signature.

model letter C.2

To the Shareholders of PQR:

Enclosed are the Annual Report for 19___, the Proxy Statement for the Annual Meeting of Shareholders and a Proxy.

The Annual Meeting of Shareholders will be held at 10:30 A.M., Tuesday, May 4, 19___ at Felt Forum, Madison Square Garden Center, 8th Avenue at 31st Street, New York, New York. You are cordially invited to be present at the Meeting. At the Meeting, shareholders will vote on

· election of directors;

· approval of appointment of independent public accountants;

· continuation of the PQR Incentive Plan as amended;

· ratification of a Nonqualified Stock Option Plan and authorization of 500,000 additional shares of Common Stock for stock option purposes;

· a resolution submitted by four shareholders concerning the PQR Incentive Plan;

· a resolution submitted by a shareholder concerning charitable contributions

and will transact any other business that may properly be brought before the Meeting.

Whether or not you expect to attend the Meeting, please fill in, sign and return the enclosed Proxy. A prompt return of your Proxy will be appreciated as it will save the expense of further mailings. In order to hold this Meeting it is necessary that the holders of a majority of the outstanding shares be present in person or represented by proxy.

If you do expect to attend the Meeting, please notify the Secretary and a card of admission will be sent to you. Proxies of shareholders who attend the Meeting and vote in person will not be voted by the Proxy Committee.

For the Board of Directors,

3. ASKING DIRECTOR IF HE WILL ATTEND THE ANNUAL MEETING

For communicating with directors who can normally be expected to attend annual meetings, the formal notices that go out with the notice of the annual meeting, the proxy, and the annual report will not suffice. A brief letter, asking only that the respondent indicate his intention of attending, will do.

General Approach

In addition to the request for information, a postage-paid envelope should be included in the letter. Some directors of companies will receive their mail at home and should be given the courtesy of prepaid postage. The actual letter should be short and complete. It may be assumed that most attendees are known to the treasurer and controller.

model letter C.3

TO:

FROM: L. A. Jones, Controller

RE: Annual Meeting of Shareholders, June 25, 19___
        10 a.m., Holiday Inn (North), Harmarville

Please indicate whether or not you will be present and return immediately. A self-addressed, stamped envelope is enclosed for your convenience.

___ I will be present.

___ I will not be present.

4. RESPONSE TO SHAREHOLDER REQUEST FOR SPECIFIC ACCOUNTING OR OTHER FINANCIAL INFORMATION

If a time ever arrives when shareholders are satisfied with the earnings of the companies in which they have invested, it will probably be just before they sell their holdings. Because most shareholders are truly concerned with "their" company, they read the annual report carefully, probably more carefully than many of the analysts who recommended the stock for purchase and who may have read mostly in the financial sections. Most shareholders are more interested in the security of their investments than they are in profitability. This is not to say that profitability is not important, but since most people buy with no intention of selling, because their purpose in buying was security, they are concerned that their investment is managed soundly.

Questions will invariably arise that will not be raised at the annual meeting, either because the questioner could not attend the meeting or because he or she was reluctant to ask the question in a public gathering. It should also be remembered that many shareholders are retired people, with little to do but to read reports concerning their investments and to think up questions that they are concerned to have answered. These same people, prior to retirement, would simply not be concerned enough to ask these questions. So, it is likely that many of the questions from shareholders will come from elderly people who are truly interested in protecting their income, which they must live on during their retirement. Treat them very gently, but firmly.

General Approach

There can be no set formula for answering a letter that contains specific questions. However, since the shareholder will likely have no source of information other than the annual report, and possibly the daily newspaper reports, the scope of questions can normally be anticipated. Whatever the question, defend the annual report, even if you disagree with some of the statements that appear in it. (It is a rare report indeed that a controller or treasurer is completely satisfied with.)

Under no conditions should any disclosures be made that do not appear in the annual report or that have not appeared in press releases issued to the public press. Anything else may lead to trouble. If in doubt, cite the particular passage in a published document; do not improvise.

A closing, as indicated here, should compliment the writer on his interest and on the rather trenchant questions he has raised. Continue on the assumption that you are dealing with a retired person (except if you know for certain otherwise, as a student who may identify himself as such) who has limited business experience, but don't let him know that that is how you feel. And always, always invite further questions as a means of forestalling further questions.

model letter C.4

Dear Mr._____:

Thank you for your inquiry regarding the President's message to shareholders in our 19__ annual report. We can appreciate your concern about the recent decline in the price of our common shares. The entire utility market has declined, as you know, from the price levels of a year ago. Both the Dow-Jones and Moody's utility averages are down 12 to 13%. The price of our shares is down about 20%. However, in April and May of this year our shares were selling at a level more than 5% above the averages and are now approximately 4% below them. Since last fall we have followed the averages very closely, sometimes rising slightly above and at other times falling a little below. Market conditions and supply and demand factors apparently cause these variations.

Now I will try to answer your two questions very specifically. First, the statement in the President's letter that "earnings are not expected to rise significantly" next year does mean what it says. We do not expect a rise of more than 5¢ to 10¢ per common share, as compared with last year's increase of 27¢ per share. As you know, rates charged for service were reduced, effective in September, and earnings in the first eight months of this year are being compared with the same period last year when rates were at the higher level.

Second, I refer you to the comments under the caption Rate Reduction on page 6 of our annual report. So long as revenues continue to rise more rapidly than plant investment the rate of return on that investment will also rise, assuming reasonable cost controls are maintained. Our book return on average net plant has increased from 5.9% to 7.3% in the last decade. In a regulated industry there is a limit to the allowed rate of return. To stay within this limit rate reductions are granted when it appears rate of return may be rising too fast. This does not mean, however, that we will not continue to have earnings growth. Such growth will be determined by the growth of our service area and the investment necessary to meet the increasing loads. Lower rates do promote use of our service, which in turn requires more investment in facilities and results in higher earnings. The future prospects for growth in our area are certainly bright, and we expect to participate fully in that growth.

We try in our reporting to be as factual as possible, often concerning complex economic matters. I hope the foregoing comments do answer your pointed and excellent questions. Thanks again for your interest and don't hesitate to contact us if we can be of further assistance.

Cordially,

5. FOLLOW-UP LETTER REQUESTING SHAREHOLDER TO SEND IN PROXY

The importance of shareholder participation in the affairs of a corporation makes mandatory some means of assuring the shareholder every opportunity to vote. In order to provide the shareholder with the feeling that he is truly important in the corporate scheme of things, it is not amiss to consider the sending of a reminder to send in a proxy if the first notice has failed to produce the desired proxy.

General Approach

As with all general letters to shareholders, the letter to be sent will appear over the signature of the president, chairman or chief executive officer, whatever his title. This follow-up letter should be sent out about two weeks before the annual meeting, about four weeks after the first proxy and annual report are sent out.

model letter C.5

A REMINDER

Dear Shareholder:

According to our latest records, we have not received your proxy for the Annual Meeting of Shareholders to be held on May 14, 19___.

Whether your holdings are large or small, the return of your signed proxy will   **(a)** be appreciated. We want all our shareholders to participate in our affairs and to vote at the meeting. The return of your proxy will not affect your right to attend the meeting and vote in person and you will be most welcome if you do attend.

For your convenience, another proxy and postpaid return envelope are enclosed. As the time before the meeting is short, I urge you to send in your proxy promptly. If you have already sent in your proxy, please disregard this letter.

Thank you for your cooperation.

Sincerely,

ALTERNATE WORDING

(a) Under the law, a certain number of shares are required for a valid election. Also, we want all our shareholders to participate in our affairs and to vote. It is not necessary to attend the meeting in person, but should you choose to attend, you may vote your shares at that time. You are most welcome to attend.

6. NOTICE TO SHAREHOLDER OF CONVERSION TO COMPUTER OPERATION

More and more companies are switching their shareholder accounting to computer operation. This enables them to include a good deal more information than they could previously have carried on dividend checks, annual statements and other documents. Since federal regulations require reporting of monies paid and received, both by the company and by the individual shareholders, these data are extremely useful and can save considerable bookkeeping effort for the company. The computer provides one solution. Some of the larger companies have already made the change, but it is likely that more and more smaller and medium-sized corporations will find that programs are available for them to utilize their existing computer facilities.

General Approach

Offer assurances that the computer will give the shareholder excellent service. That this will not always be the case is going to become apparent enough, particularly since errors of the sort made as a result of errors in input to the computer can lead to wrong dividend amounts, inability of the postman to deliver the mail to a mis-addressed location, etc.

With these aspects so evident, the letter writer is under obligation to his shareholder to ask him to make corrections in the data. Even with the most careful system, experts have estimated the number of items with errors to be one in ten. This means that one error, major or minor, could occur in some place in the form. With recipient verification, errors could be reduced to only one in 100, a much more acceptable level. Some errors are likely to persist, even though efforts are made to incorporate all corrections and changes.

model letter C.6

To the Shareholders:

We have completed conversion of our shareholder records system to computer operation. We are confident that this advanced system will provide an efficient, accurate service to our shareholders.

The enclosed dividend check is the first to be issued utilizing the new system.

We suggest that you take this opportunity to inspect your name and address and advise us of any appropriate changes by using the space available on the face of the check.

Provision has also been made on the check for your taxpayer's identifying number which is normally a shareholder's Social Security number. Please review the number for accuracy, or indicate the number if none appears on the check.

Sincerely,

group D

DEALINGS RELATING
TO SECURITIES

Dealings Relating to Securities

Every public corporation has dealings relating to the securities of the company, normally securities traded on a recognized securities exchange or in an organized fashion over-the-counter. Laws being what they are, the securities that are issued by a company, generally in the form of stocks and bonds, must be approved prior to issue by the Securities and Exchange Commission. If the securities are traded on an exchange, the manner in which they are handled, traded, bought, sold, discussed, etc., are also governed by the rules of the various exchanges. In a few special cases, such as in the New York Stock Exchange, the rules governing the disclosure of information are those that were in force at the time the various securities were entered for trading. Of course, if a later issue were entered, the most stringent rules affecting one issue would apply to all issues of the company. As a rule, however, all companies generally tend to try to conform with the highest disclosure and practice standards set by the NYSE, standards that are usually higher than even those of the SEC.

All matters relating to the buying, selling, "touting" or transfer of securities of a publicly held corporation are a matter of record. To assure that all matters are handled in a discreet manner and that they comply with appropriate regulations, it is extremely desirable to reduce all communication to written form. In this instance, the written letter provides the company with protection against misrepresentation and suspicion.

1. Covering Letter for Financial Data Transmitted to Securities and Exchange Commission

A covering letter, this is a formal transmission of data that are required by regulations of the Securities and Exchange Commission. It should be sent via certified mail to assure the date of receipt.

General Approach

In dealing with government agencies, it is desirable to add a reference. This follows the style of Government communications and is well understood by federal agencies. It is the style recommended by the Style Manual of the Government Printing Office; it is also the style used in correspondence by and with many state and local government agencies.

Just to make certain that the information being transmitted is understood to meet the specific requirments, it is always advisable to indicate the nature of the enclosure. Should the enclosure become separated from the letter, as it later will, it will be possible to trace the letter and its contents at any subsequent date, should that become necessary.

model letter D.1

Re: The ABC Corporation
       Commission File No. 0-2626

Dear Sirs:

We are transmitting herewith three (3) fully executed copies of the company's current report on Form 8-K for the month of November, 19___.

Very truly yours,

2. Covering Letter for Transmittal of Reports That Are Also Sent to Shareholders

The Securities and Exchange Commission requires notice that the procedures required by the SEC and the law are followed properly. The matter of transmittal of information to the shareholders is one such matter. The SEC stands as the guardian of the rights of shareholders and can, if it sees fit, suspend the rights of management to protect those of the shareholders. The SEC must be kept informed of actions that affect the shareholders and their rights. Not only, in this case, does indication of the intentions of the management to transmit the annual report or other reports have to be given, but some evidence that actual transmittal took place must exist if demanded later by the SEC.

General Approach

Reference to the subject is an essential part of the opening of the letter. Reference to the Commission file number is extremely desirable, particularly since every company that has publicly issued securities has such a number. This does make the task of the SEC easier, and it eliminates the risk of confusion, which management always wishes to avoid.

The style of the letter is terse, and it gives only the information absolutely necessary to assure that the recipient of the letter knows the actions and intentions of the sender.

The closing is courteous but businesslike and is signed in the name of the corporation.

model letter D.2

Re: ABC Corporation
     Annual Report—19___
     Commission File No. 0-1234

Gentlemen:

We have enclosed eight (8) copies of the Annual Report for the year ended **(a)** December 31, 19___.

Copies of the report are to be mailed to the shareholders the week of **(b)** March 31, 19___.

The record date is April 18, 19___.

Sincerely yours,

Alternate Wording

(a) We have enclosed eight (8) copies of the Second Quarter Report for the six months ending June 30, 19___.

(b) Copies of this report were mailed to the shareholders the week of August 11, 19___.

3. COVERING LETTER FOR FINANCIAL AND OTHER DATA TRANSMITTED TO THE GOVERNORS OF EXCHANGES ON WHICH STOCK OF THE COMPANY IS TRADED

Three letters are shown here to indicate the nature of communications to, in this case, the American Stock Exchange. In the first letter, a record of transmittal of a report is made. Filing of the annual report, and other periodic fiscal reports, is required under the rules of various securities exchanges. The rules differ from one exchange to another, and even within the same exchange depending upon the agreement in force at the time the stock of the company was admitted to trading. Nevertheless, certain rules of practice are considered conventional. One of these is that all reports filed with the Securities and Exchange Commission are sent to the exchange. The first letter is identical in form to the letter sent to the SEC.

The second letter contains information for the records of the exchange. It is short and to the point. Since the likelihood of personal acquaintance of the writer with the recipients of the letter is slight, there is no need for personal comments. This letter covers all points of information; no superfluous information not directly related to the purpose of the communication is required.

The third letter notifies the Exchange of the intentions of the management of the company to hold their annual meeting. It confirms the intentions of the management to keep the Exchange properly informed.

model letter D.3A

Re: ABC Corporation
Annual Report—19___.

Dear Mr._____

We have enclosed six (6) copies of the Annual Report for the year ended **(a)**
December 31, 19___.

Copies of the report are to be mailed to the shareholders the week of **(b)**
March 31, 19___.

The record date is April 18, 19___.

Very truly yours,

ALTERNATE WORDING

(a) We have enclosed six (6) copies of the Second Quarter Report for the six months ending June 30, 19__.

(b) Copies of this report were mailed to the shareholders the week of August 11, 19__.

model letter D.3B

Re: Annual Meeting of Shareholders, June 25, 19__.

Dear Mr._____ :

The Directors of the Company elected at the annual meeting of Shareholders held on June 25, 19__, for the following year as follows:

> Andrew N. Jones
> Vincent J. Smith
> Alfonso J. Cohen
> August A. Gale
> Joseph L. Palmer
> Morris D. Rush
> J. G. Schirmer
> Mario T. Vincent

The Officers of the Company elected at the June 25, 19__ meeting of the Board of Directors for the following year are as follows:

Andrew N. Jones	Chairman of the Board and President
Vincent J. Smith	Executive Vice President, Assistant Secretary and Assistant Treasurer
J. G. Schirmer	Secretary and Treasurer
Steve T. Lake	Vice President, Purchasing

Very truly yours,

model letter D.3c

Dear Mr._____:

The annual meeting of shareholders will be held June 25, 19___. A copy of the official "Notice of Annual Meeting of Shareholders" will be mailed to your office in due time.

The record date is April 18, 19___.

Very truly yours,

4. NOTICE TO SECURITIES AND EXCHANGE COMMISSION OF CHANGE IN OWNERSHIP OF CORPORATE SHARES BY CORPORATE OFFICER

Under the present regulations, officers of corporations may make purchases of shares of stock of the company under certain specified conditions. Beneficial ownership of such shares presumes the hope, not the fact, of corporate growth and prosperity sometime in the future, and also presumes that the action of the corporate officer cannot be construed as a speculation. Nevertheless, the Securities and Exchange Commission requires that any changes in stock ownership be placed on record with them. Purchases of corporate stock for the account of the officer of the company fall into a different category and are governed by different regulations.

General Approach

Since the reporting of the change is all that is required, as a distinction from obtaining permission in advance of making a change in stock ownership, a brief covering letter is all that is required. A standard form, available from the SEC, is filled out with the pertinent information.

All such correspondence with the SEC should be sent by certified mail, not registered mail, with return receipt requested. This is to assure the proof of arrival of the information. The receipt is then filed with the copy of the covering letter against future calls, if any.

model letter D.4

CERTIFIED MAIL
RETURN RECEIPT REQUESTED

Attention: Division of Corporate Finance

Re: The ABC Corporation
      File No. 0-2762
      Form 4—January, 19___.

Gentlemen:

We are transmitting herewith one (1) fully executed copy of SEC Form 4—
Statement of Changes in Beneficial Ownership of Securities for James E.
McFarland.

Very truly yours,

5. Rejecting an Invitation of a Security Analysts' Group to Speak Before the Group

When rejecting an invitation to speak before a group of security analysts, it must be made perfectly clear why the invitation is being rejected. Any inference that the company wishes to avoid publicizing information that might be construed as un-complimentary to the company will be received in precisely that way, and will cause an unfavorable reaction. A rejection must be expressed clearly and unequivocally. Reasons for rejection have to be spelled out.

Among the many reasons for rejecting an invitation is the desire to avoid excessive exposure. As a matter of policy, most companies wish to maintain a balance of appearances, making neither too few nor too many. Of course, companies that are in the public eye or that seem to be of special interest to analysts for various reasons will be asked to make more appearances than they might prefer. When an invitation is rejected, the door should be left open to an acceptance sometime in the future. Anything else would be insulting, and this cannot be permitted to occur.

New action on the part of a company will tend to stimulate interest by analysts, particularly if the action could affect the market for securities of the company. Since the function of security analysts is to provide, among other things, appraisals of the value of the securities offered to the public, actions of the company that will affect the value of existing public issues will be of interest to the analysts. New issues, rumors of splits, additional offerings, etc., all tend to stimulate the appetites of analysts' groups for more detailed information. When any of these situations are in limbo, it is necessary to avoid making appearances. A letter rejecting an invitation to speak is then in order.

General Approach

This letter, from a Fortune 500 Company, indicates a typical situation. Its stock is traded on the New York Stock Exchange. The company is involved in new technologies, acquisitions and negotiations for new acquisitions and other situations that make its stock potentially more volatile and of greater public interest than the securities of most other companies. Since companies in this position will most frequently be asked to have speakers appear before interested groups of analysts, the letter rejecting the invitation must very carefully spell out the reasons for rejection and promise the analysts the opportunity to enjoy a presentation in the reasonably near future.

model letter D.5

Dear Mr._____:

Thank you for your invitation addressed to our chairman, John Doe, to appear **(a)**
next month before the Los Angeles Society of Security Analysts. Unfortunately,
we have just completed a presentation before the Chicago Society, and, as
you may recall, we appeared only last January 29th in San Francisco. With
very little new to say, we feel that this is not a particularly opportune time to
appear before your group, especially since the proceedings of both of the other
meetings have been published.

We, as a matter of general practice, ordinarily like to appear before about three **(b)**
major analysts' societies across the country during a given year. It would seem
as if we should be thinking about appearing in Los Angeles sometime during
the winter or early Spring of 19__. If this fits conveniently into your schedule,
I'm sure we would be much more amenable to the idea at that time.

Our company is very anxious to cooperate with all interested investment **(c)**
groups, and I certainly hope we'll be able to work out a satisfactory time to make
the appearance before your important organization.

Sincerely,

ALTERNATE WORDING

(a) Thank you for your invitation to appear before your Society of Security
Analysts. As you know, our company has a request for the issuance of a

new stock issue pending with the SEC. Under the circumstances, we would consider it inadvisable to have a representative of our company make an appearance before your group at this time.

(a) Thank you for your kind invitation addressed to our chairman, John Doe, to appear next month before your local chapter of the Society of Security Analysts. We feel that the invitation should be extended to the chairman of our financial committee, Mr. Robert Roe, who has willingly given of his time in the past to meet with members of the financial community.

(b) As a general practice, we prefer to have analysts visit our offices and plants where we are able to assemble groups of key corporate management personnel. This gives the analysts an opportunity to ask questions of and to obtain answers from company officials, first hand, who would not normally attend meetings of the type your group holds.

(c) Should you find it possible for your membership to arrange to be away from their offices, we would be pleased to arrange a tour of our facilities and have them join with our management at a luncheon meeting. At the meeting, we would entertain questions relating to the visit and to the company's business. Please let me know what dates you would want to consider and approximately how many of your members would be involved.

6. Answering Questions of Broker or Security Analyst Concerning Future Growth and Stock Improvement Potentials of Company

Every broker or security analyst seems to have a particular area of interest within the general scope of his interest in an industry or company. He will have found a point that he feels gives him a special and personal insight into the total market and that, if he pursues it, will provide him with sufficient data to make reasonable judgments. As a result, even though a complete presentation is given on a topic in a public forum, expanded notes are frequently needed for a special analyst or broker who is considered important to a controller or treasurer of a company for the influence he has on the market for the company's securities.

General Approach

The letter shown here provides just such an expansion upon a topic, covering specific points that had been raised by an analyst. An effort must be made at all costs to avoid disclosing information to one analyst that has not already been made available to all other interested persons and analysts, the general public included. It might otherwise be misconstrued as providing special information to a specific person for a personal reason of the correspondent.

The author of this letter deliberately took pains to quote from a document that has or will have received wide distribution. He has extracted excerpts from this document to provide answers to his questioner, but he has not added any new information or facts. It is reasonable to express opinions concerning business prospects, but these should be very, very carefully worded and should be backed up with facts, as indeed this author has done.

A letter is a safer means of providing such information than a telephone conversation. Conversation can easily get out of bounds of propriety; a letter can be reviewed to avoid this possibility. Answers to queries by analysts and brokers should therefore be committed to writing to avoid the possibility of letting an impropriety slip by.

model letter D.6

Dear Mr._____:

Thanks for your telephone call yesterday afternoon. Perhaps it will be beneficial if I expand on the points we discussed.

First of all, here are some excerpts of Carlson Bennett's remarks at the Chicago   **(a)**
Society Meeting in answer to a question from the floor on the economy and the housing market. (The speech and the complete Q&A are in the process of distribution, but you may not have received them yet.) Carl's remarks are remarkably close to those of the ABC Co. officer.

". . . Housing's history since World War II has followed the same pattern on several occasions. Its growth peaked and started to decline before the general economy peaked, and housing has always started to rebound before the general economy reached its trough. We have seen what to us looks like firming at levels which are not as low as those experienced during the dip in housing of the 19___–19___ period. Housing starts are at a higher level than they were then. As most of you all know, in the last two months at least, the inflow into the thrift institutions, such as savings and loan associations, has risen rather sharply.

We feel that with the measures that have at long last been taken by the Federal Government, highlighted by the Federal Home Loan Bank Board, asking, in effect, the savings and loan companies not to repay their outstanding loans, and giving them something of a subsidy on the interest rates they pay on them, should lead to a recovery in housing during the second half. It is entirely possible that the fourth quarter could well close at an annual rate of 1.6 million to 1.7 million units. If that is the case, and barring unforeseen events, there should be a very healthy effect on the housing industry and on the building material suppliers with a very good year in 19___. We have had some increase in basic commodity plywood prices in March and April. Standard has not held as firm, but that is the smallest part of it. Sheathing, which is the largest part, has held rather firmly. The prices are not at the moment rising, but they are not slipping."

As I mentioned, perhaps 1.5 and 1.6 million starts at the end of the year rather than 1.7 is a little more realistic, but it's all a matter of the rate of rise and when it begins. Whatever that rate is, it's seasonally adjusted, and doesn't mean much for this year's business, but it does set the stage for a good level of business next year.

As far as commodity plywood price levels are concerned, we don't believe a 1.8 or 1.9 million housing start figure is necessary to firm our prices at a satisfactory level, although we'd be delighted to see that level of building activity. As you know, we have very tight belts, have been concentrating on operating efficiency, and we could make very satisfactory profit levels with plywood price levels in the mid-80's and up. I think our people feel that total housing in 19__ of around 1.6 million or so would bring about such satisfactory price levels. I'm attaching a rough listing of plywood prices over the past two years, which will give you an idea of just what we're talking about.

Your calls and short notes are always interesting and helpful to us, and we're delighted to have the opportunity to trade information with you whenever we have the chance. I hope this is of some help.

Regards,

ALTERNATE WORDING

In place of any paragraph except the closing paragraph, the following may be used:

(a) As you realize, I cannot give you any information that has not already been made available to the general public, either in the form of a talk or as a published set of comments. However, I would like to bring your attention to the comments of our chairman as they are currently being published. I shall underline, in the copy I transmit to you, the answer to the specific points about which you inquired.

7. REFUSING REQUEST BY SECURITY ANALYST TO MAKE PLANT TOUR OR HAVE PERSONAL INTERVIEW

Any controller or treasurer who permits an analyst to visit his plant or offices for a discussion of "prospects" while registration of a securities issue is pending is likely to find himself facing the Securities and Exchange Commission. Likewise, any broker or analyst who knowingly makes such a visit is certainly opening the door to punitive measures. This letter is a definite and firm refusal to permit an analyst to make a visit of a private, apparently confidential nature. It keeps the door open to a visit in a public area, during which private business will, presumably, not be discussed.

General Approach

The writer acknowledges the request for a visit, which in this instance was made by telephone. Because analysts generally try to combine meetings with other business (as do most businessmen), it seems natural to schedule such a visit at the same time as a business meeting or convention.

The second paragraph indicates the writer's reason for his apparent reluctance to commit himself over the telephone.

In the third paragraph, the writer has noted that he is acting upon the advice of counsel in refusing the visit. SEC regulations are sufficiently clear for him to have dispensed with questioning the company's legal department; he should have known this without question or should have taken this step as a matter of normal precaution.

model letter D.7

Dear Mr._____:

This is following up your telephone call to me, at which time you asked if our representatives who will be in the City for the due diligence meeting, February 8, could visit you for a separate and personal interview.

I guess you were aware of a certain vagueness in my response to this request. I should have asked you then if you knew that we were in registration for an issue of 1,400,000 shares of Common Stock as well as the $25,000,000 Bond issue. This occasioned my hesitancy in replying to your request.

I have discussed this matter and have been counseled that, in view of the **(a)** Common issue, we should not indulge in any such interview as you contemplate. I do hope, however, that you will be present at the technical meeting and that I may have a chance to visit with you then. Later on, I shall be most happy **(b)** to visit with you concerning our business and the prospects in store for us. Incidentally, I mentioned to Bill Jones that you had called and he spoke very highly of you personally and as one of the leaders in your field. I should appreciate it if you would look me up at the meeting.

With best regards.

ALTERNATE WORDING

The second paragraph does not need the first or third sentences. They relate to a personal relationship, which may be lacking in other correspondence. The second sentence, giving the respondent the reason for the refusal, is sufficient to stand by itself. The third paragraph should be separated into two paragraphs, and could read:

(a) In view of the Common issue, we should not indulge in any such interview as you contemplate.

(b) Later on, after completion of the issue, I shall be happy to visit with you or have you visit with us concerning our business and the future prospects.

8. RESPONDING TO A REPORT OR COMMENTS MADE BY A SECURITY ANALYST

Annual reports are a source of headaches for controllers, analysts and others. They seem invariably to be less complete or less detailed, or less something-or-other than everyone would like. In short, they please nobody completely. This letter is in response to a "complaint" by and suggestions of a security analyst—possibly for methods of improving the report.

General Approach

With few exceptions, an analyst who writes to criticize an annual report is someone who is known to the controller or treasurer; so a first-name salutation is not out of order. If the person is just recently acquainted, a more formal opening may be suitable.

The first paragraph relates to the effort of the analyst in going through the report and in writing or telephoning his criticisms to the controller. Most likely, the comments are in a letter, to which this letter is the response.

The closing refers to the personal meeting of the analyst with the controller.

model letter D.8

Dear Don:

I want to thank you for the time you gave to my Annual Report project and,   **(a)**
as I told you, I appreciate sincerely your constructive criticism. I do not anticipate
that I will incorporate all of your suggestions since that would be abdicating
my prerogatives. I do propose, however, giving serious consideration to using
most of them.

(b)

It was pleasurable visiting with you both in New York and Philadelphia and   **(c)**
I look forward to the next opportunity.

Sincerely,

ALTERNATE WORDING

(a) I want to thank you for the time and effort you have given to my Annual
Report. I appreciate sincerely your constructive criticism. Since I have not
yet had the opportunity to review all your comments with my staff, I shall
have to reserve comment on our ability to incorporate these ideas into our
next report.

(b) As you know, our annual reports are the work of a large group of people,
some of whom have rather strong opinions concerning the content and tone
of the report. I shall present your ideas, without expressing my own opinions,
to enable our Report committee to pass upon them concerning the desira-
bility of using them in future reports.

(c) I look forward to meeting with you again in the near future.

9. THANKING AN ANALYST FOR A VISIT

This type of letter is a formality and should definitely be written any time an
analyst takes the time to hear your presentation, in any form, or visits your company's
premises at your invitation. The value of the visit is apparent enough, or why have
such a visit, either by him or by you? The value of the thank you letter should be
obvious, especially since it takes so little time and effort. A typical "thank you"
letter is shown.

model letter D.9

Dear Mr._____:

It was a pleasure to meet with you last week. I enjoyed the luncheon and the
good conversation. This is to express my appreciation and thanks.

Please give me a call when you are in the downtown area so that we may
have lunch together again.

Cordially,

10. Transmittal of Copy of Talk Given Before a Group of Controllers, Analysts, or even the Local Chamber of Commerce

Organizations of controllers, analysts (or even local chambers of commerce or Lions clubs) have publications in which they publish copies of talks given at their membership meetings. It is their desire to bring the talk to all those members who were unable to attend or to those who were at the meeting and wish to go over specific points of the talk in detail.

The sample letter encompasses one such covering letter. In the covering letter, the background information about the speaker is noted. This is usually important because the introductory remarks at the meeting tend often to be less complete than they would be for a more formal, printed presentation.

In transmitting a copy of a talk, or a summary of such a talk, the writer should be careful to edit the material to eliminate references to slides that are not included in the written text as illustrations, and to avoid comments that are suited only to oral presentation. He should also provide a very clean copy. The editors of such organization journals are seldom professional editors and unwanted comments may find their way into print.

General Approach

Since the speaker is generally known personally to the person who makes the request for the material for publication, the use of first names is acceptable. The actual transmittal should specify the date and circumstances of the talk to avoid confusion with other times and places.

model letter D.10

Dear Mr._____:

As promised, I have enclosed a brief summary of my talk before the Metropolitan Controllers Association on the evening of May 15, 19___. In addition, I have enclosed the background information about myself that you had requested.

With best regards,

11. Request for Clarification of Accounting Requirements of the New York Stock Exchange (or other Exchange)

As business conditions change, and they do constantly, requirements of companies to provide certain accounting data change too. In particular, companies that are listed or desire to become listed on various stock exchanges will find that their accounting disclosure practices are not always in accord with the desires and requirements of the exchange. Therefore, it becomes necessary for them to ascertain what the current acceptable accounting practices are.

Of particular interest, because they affect shareholders, are statements and pronouncements of companies concerning their earnings per share. Practices in this regard are sometimes more strictly prescribed by the exchange than by a regulatory agency, such as the SEC. It is likely that the exchange will have some "opinions"— as the recommendations of the NYSE are called.

Many of these opinions cover far more than a single subject, as, for instance, Opinion No. 9, which covers matters relating to financial statements, interim reports, annual reports, etc.

In practice, the New York Stock Exchange does not promulgate accounting rules or state opinions concerning such rules as may be enunciated by the Accounting Principles Board, whose rulings it accepts. Because reporting requirements are established for each listed company on the basis of the requirements current at the time of listing, the NYSE generally tries to bring all reports of its member companies to the same standard of completeness and clarity.

General Approach

A straightforward approach is most useful for this type of letter. The NYSE, for instance, is forthright about its responses and gives the same answers to all respondents. Certainly, a request for information will be followed by a response that is most complete and will likely cover many matters not considered in the original letter of request.

Depending upon the relationship of the company's controller or treasurer with the personnel of the exchange (whether listed or hope-to-be-listed), the person addressed will vary. If listed, the individual may be someone with whom the controller or treasurer has had considerable contact concerning his stock. Most likely, it will be the Executive Accountant. If not a listed company, the writer would likely address his letter to the Vice-President in Charge of Listings.

model letter D.11

Dear Mr._____:

Could you please indicate those accounting practices that are most acceptable   **(a)**
to the New York Stock Exchange. It is our understanding that the authoritative
method is that prescribed by the Accounting Principles Board.

We have found in our files a number of letters and opinions from the NYSE
covering the matter of clarification of accounting practices and indication that

additional accounting information is desired in certain specified areas. It seems, or that is our understanding, that such opinions go beyond the basic financial statements, such as are audited by independent public accountants, and that these opinions also extend to interim reports, narrative sections of annual reports, and other publications of member companies relating to earnings-per-share data.

We would be pleased to hear from you regarding these matters.

Sincerely,

ALTERNATE WORDING

(a) We are engaged in a research effort relative to interim financial reporting and are seeking the New York Stock Exchange's requirements in this respect.

INSURANCE PROBLEMS

Insurance Problems

Insurance is basically a financial operation involving, as it does, the relationship of cost of product versus the cost of protecting the investment made in the product. As such, it is normally handled by the controller or treasurer. As values change, the amount of money invested in insurance must change accordingly. As inventory changes, so do insurance needs, and so forth.

The specialized nature of insurance frequently, and especially in large companies, requires the full-time services of an insurance specialist. A smaller company may use a consultant or may rely upon an insurance broker to anticipate its needs. When a company institutes an employee insurance plan, it is customary to notify the employees by mail, usually at their homes, and it is usually the fiscal officer who writes the letter, even if the president signs it. Insurance affecting employees is a rather personal matter and should be treated as such.

The following letters represent some of the more frequently encountered situations concerning insurance.

model letter E.1

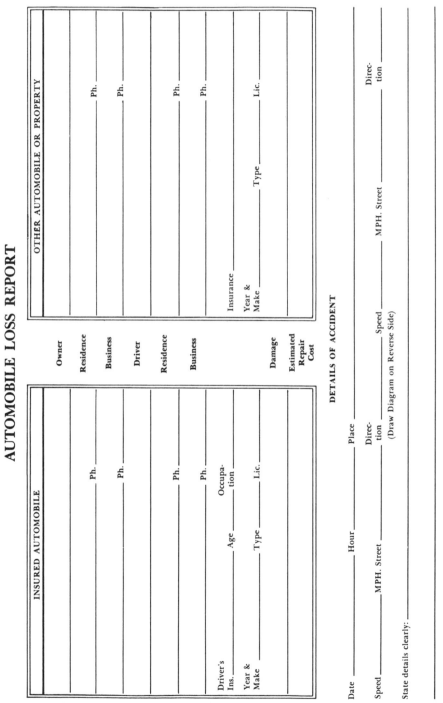

Police   Yes
Report?   No   No. _____

Copy
Requested _____

Charged: Insured
Other _____   Violation _____

INJURED	1. In Ins'd Car, Other, or Ped.	2. In Ins'd Car, Other, or Ped.	3. In Ins'd Car, Other, or Ped.
Name			
Address			
Phone	_____ Age	_____ Age	_____ Age
Injuries			
Taken To			

WITNESS	1. In Ins'd Car, Other, or Ped.	2. In Ins'd Car, Other, or Ped.	3. In Ins'd Car, Other, or Ped.
Name			
Address & Phone			

Reported by: Insured, Agent   Received by _____   Date _____

DO NOT WRITE IN SPACES BELOW. FOR HOME OFFICE USE ONLY.

	RESV.	COLL. DED.	BI LIMITS	IS.	SD	SUB.	PD LIMITS	MP LIMITS	COMP.	U.M. LIMITS	LIAB.	SYM.	C/L
(1)													
(2)													
(3)													

	MAJ.	MIN.	ASSN. CLASS	CO. CODE	A/C #	REINS.	CODE	AGENTS NAME	AGE
(1)									
(2)									
(3)									

CL 416C 2/67

1. NOTICE TO INSURANCE BROKER OR COMPANY REPRESENTATIVE OF INSURED LOSS

Depending upon the size of a company and its insurable properties, it will employ either the services of an insurance broker or will deal directly with the insurance companies. In either instance, when an insured loss occurs, the broker or company will have to be notified. A very large corporation or one that uses a large number of company-owned vehicles may have its own forms, which it uses to transmit details of an insured loss to an insurance company.

The sample form is used for such reporting. It even contains provision for the agent's name, among other details. (See sample form, pages 116 and 117.)

General Approach

The operator of the vehicle fills out the details of the automobile loss form. This is in addition to any other forms required by state or local law. This record is kept in duplicate and serves the usual purpose of such forms.

2. REQUEST TO INSURANCE COMPANY FOR PAYMENT FOR ADJUSTED LOSS

Once an insurance loss has been adjusted, there should be little reason for delay in payment. Just as an individual has to conform to the legal requirements to make accident reports, file claims and obtain estimates, so do the same rules apply to corporations, companies and other business entities. In those states in which compulsory insurance laws apply, the request for payment is made to the insurance company. In those states in which voluntary insurance laws apply, the initial request for payment is made to an individual or company whose fault was established. However, once an insurance company enters the case, the claim for payment is made to the insurance company acting in behalf of its assured.

Although the example here refers to a claim for automobile damage, it could easily refer to any other type of adjusted loss.

General Approach

All insurance companies maintain a claim file, which is the complete file of all correspondence, records and other matters relating to the particular incident. Reference to the claim number is the first item of information needed by the insurance company. Reference to the name of the assured serves as a further reference. The amount need not be mentioned at this point, but it serves no harm to call attention to the amount to alert the insurance company to the type of treatment they should accord the claim for damages. A small amount receives much more rapid handling than does a claim for a large sum of money. The individual to whom the letter is addressed is probably the person who sent notice to the claimant—in this case, the company—that the insurance company wished to receive a certified statement of the amount of the damages.

Reiteration of the circumstances of the accident is useful. The fact that the company has made an investigation may or may not be germane to any particular situation. Usually, a company does not make its own investigation, but states, as in the preceding paragraph, the circumstances surrounding the reason for the claim.

Asking for payment is the purpose of the letter and is, of course, appropriate. The closing is courteous in that it indicates that the claimant does not hold the insurance company responsible for the actions of its assured but does hold them accountable for payment of damages incurred by their assureds.

model letter E.2

Re: Claim
      Your Insured:
      Our Property Damage: $143.74

Dear Mr._____:

We have enclosed copies of the report of Motor Vehicle accident sent to our **(a)** insurance company and the estimate of repairs to our company vehicle, a Buick, which was struck, while parked on Massachusetts Avenue, Arlington, Massachusetts, by your insured's car.

Our investigation indicates that this damage was the result of your insured's negligence.

Please forward your draft in the amount of $143.74 to The ABC Company as **(b)** soon as possible.

Your early attention to this matter will be appreciated.

Very truly yours,

ALTERNATE WORDING

(a) In accordance with the estimate of loss made by your adjuster, we request that payment be made of the amount, agreed upon verbally and confirmed above, as soon as possible. Prompt payment will enable us to make restitution of facilities as soon as possible and allow us to resume full operation.

With this optional paragraph, eliminate the second paragraph in the sample letter.

(b) Enclosed is a copy of an estimate of the cost of repairs from a reliable repair service recommended by your company.

3. MAKING CLAIM FOR DAMAGE AGAINST CARRIER

Loss and damage claims are standard problems encountered by every business. Claims are filed on standard forms, some of which can be purchased from office-supply houses. Others are printed up by the company for their own use. It is not generally necessary to have a letter of transmittal since the form has all details listed.

The processing time of many claims brings them well beyond the normal 30-day accounting period. In particular, a claim for payment by a carrier may be sent by the carrier to its insurance company. The value may be sufficiently large to justify a detailed investigation. These require considerable time because nobody is about to rush into closing a case without thorough study. As a matter of course, a follow-up letter would be sent to the carrier some months after the claim has been filed, asking for payment or for a reason for not yet settling.

General Approach

A simple form note is all that is necessary to remind the carrier of his obligation to honor the claim made on him.

model letter E.3

(with attached form on page 121)

Gentlemen:

When may we expect to receive settlement of the enclosed subject claim, or reason why payment is being withheld?   **(a)**

An early reply is requested.

Very truly yours,

ALTERNATE WORDING

(a) As a result of loss (damage) to our property while in your care, we are making claim for loss as indicated on the enclosed form.

LOSS and DAMAGE CLAIM

This claim payable to ABC Company _____ for $235.28 is made for loss ___ damage ___ on the following described shipment:

35 Coils Soft Copper Water Tube, 2800 lbs.

CONSIGNOR	ABC Company	**ORIGIN**	Bridgeport, Connecticut
CONSIGNEE	XYZ Company	**DESTINATION**	Buffalo, New York
CAR INITIAL & NO.		**F/B NO.**	05-555-555
ROUTE	ABC Trucking Line	**DATE SHIPPED**	5/22/19__

DETAIL STATEMENT SHOWING HOW AMOUNT CLAIM IS DETERMINED

7 coils 2″ Type K Soft x 40 ft. — 280 ft. @ 1.761 per ft. $493.08

less Scrap Value 7 coils, 80 lbs. per coil — 560 lbs. @ .46 per lb.   257.60

Total Amount Claimed $235.48

DOCUMENTS SUBMITTED

(x) 1. Original bill of lading.
(x) 2. Original paid freight bill.
(x) 3. Original invoice or certified copy.

(x) 4. Copy of carrier's inspection report.
( ) 5. O.S.&D. Report
( ) 6.

REMARKS:

INDEMNITY AGREEMENT

We hereby agree to protect the carrier and its connections against any loss by reason of our being unable to produce the Original Freight Bill and/or Bill of Lading or both.

CERTIFICATION OF VALUE

"We hereby certify the foregoing statement of facts is correct and that the prices used in this claim is/are the due date destination value in the quantity shipped."

ABC Company

Company

Claimant's Signature

4. LETTER TO CUSTOMER OR CARRIER REFUSING TO ACCEPT RESPONSIBILITY FOR SHIPPING DAMAGE OR LOSS

It matters little to the supplier of goods whether a shortage is the result of improper handling at the receiving end or improper handling by the carrier. In either situation, he is entitled to payment, with claims for loss to be adjudicated between the recipient named on the bill of lading and the transfer agent or shipping company. Most shipments of goods are made F.O.B. shipping point. Thus, the carrier becomes the agent of the purchaser. In the event the carrier is named by the purchaser as being his preferred carrier there is no question that liability for the loss cannot lie with the shipper and rests with the recipient of the goods. If the shipper selects the carrier, the question is not always quite as easily resolved.

General Approach

Since claims for losses must be filed as soon as possible, it is necessary for the claimant to have proof of the value of the merchandise and proof of shipment. This is provided by the shipper. When a claim is made, the shipper should cooperate by sending copies of those papers that prove that the carrier's employee or agent actually accepted the goods in good condition.

The shipper is entitled to payment just as if the merchandise had been received; for, in fact, it was received by the carrier. He should recommend the immediate filing of claim for loss, damage or shortage. If not, he may still stand to lose all or part of the value of the merchandise in question.

model letter E.4

Attn: Manager Accounts Payable Dept.

Gentlemen:

We are attaching a copy of our invoice number 09690 of December 5, 19___ for $159.32 and a copy of the bill of lading covering shipment.

You claim a shortage of 4 blankets on this shipment and since our terms are **(a)** F.O.B. Shipping Point, we will appreciate your mailing us your check and filing claim with Pilot Freight Carriers for this shortage.

We suggest that you file this claim as soon as possible since the statute of limitations on payment of claims by the carrier terminates nine months from date of shipment.

Very truly yours,

ALTERNATE WORDING

(a) Before we can estimate the cost of repairs, we would have to examine the equipment in detail. This would require us to send a skilled technician to your plant, the services of whom would be covered in your claim to the carrier.

(a) The damage to the merchandise (equipment) appears to have resulted from improper storage, transit or handling by the freight forwarder and/or his agents. This being the case, we suggest that you file your claim with the forwarder and carrier for the amount you determine to be necessary to effect complete repair or replacement of the merchandise (equipment).

5. REQUEST TO INSURANCE COMPANY TO ACCOUNT FOR METHOD OF INVOICING FOR INSURANCE

Each year, insurance premiums must be audited where the insurance premium is determined by the experience of the company, as with workmen's compensation insurance. In this letter, the writer is asking the insurance company to verify and account for the amount of its invoice for the year. In some ways, the request for this accounting is not unlike the request for verification of any invoice; a detailed accounting is desired.

General Approach

Initially, the receipt of the invoice is acknowledged. Following that, the writer asks for the details he feels may significantly affect the amount of the invoice. The closing is a courteous promise to process the invoice as soon as the requested information is received.

model letter E.5

Attention: Mr. W. Garner, Special Risk Dept.

Gentlemen:

We received your invoice for the final audit on our Workmen's Compensation Policy for the year 19___.

We would appreciate receiving a detailed analysis as to how the amount shown was determined. In other words, the total payroll for the year, the effective rates, the total premium as computed, the amounts paid on the account, the application of the 15% dividend and all other factors which went into making up this final figure.

Upon receiving this information we shall process your invoice.

Very truly yours,

group F

MERGERS, ACQUISITIONS
AND CHANGES IN
CORPORATE NAME

Mergers, Acquisitions and Changes in Corporate Name

In an era of mergers, spin-offs, consolidations, acquisitions and just simple changes in names for new corporate identity, the amount of correspondence relating to changes in name has become significant. Changes in name are major undertakings and are done only when either the market or financial structure make it necessary.

Changes in corporate name involve customers, suppliers, bankers and other loan institutions. They will certainly affect the public image because, unless tremendous effort is made to inform the general public, the new name has to become accepted with its new corporate image. Arrangements to notify the public are handled by extensive public relations and advertising programs by other corporate officials; arrangements affecting fiscal relationships are handled by the controller, treasurer or similar high-ranking corporate fiscal officer.

1. Notifying Customers of Acquisition by or of Another Company

The acquisition of one company by another is a signal for customers of the acquired company to be notified that they can continue to do business with the old firm, but under a new corporate name or management. Also, they should be given to believe that the merger will benefit them because of combined facilities, which will offer them improvement in service as well as in accounting procedures. The letter to the customers will be written by the acquiring company to the new list of customers it has obtained, as well as to its own customer list.

If the acquired company is to remain autonomous, the letter will reflect that fact by noting the continuity of personnel and places of business. If the acquired company is to be integrated within the acquiring company, changes in places and methods of doing business should be very specifically noted. The same letter will be sent by the company whether it has been acquired or has done the acquiring, since the net effect is the same for either action insofar as the customer is concerned. Also, it is now the combined company that sends out the announcement, so the distinction of acquirer or acquiree is immaterial.

General Approach

Assume the merger or acquisition is known to the customer. Since they will have been doing business with the acquired firm, they would likely have been informed of the move by sales personnel who call on them or even by the industry grapevine or public-relations announcements. Since the merger has come about because the managements of both companies believe it to be in the best interests of both companies, they can point with pride at the possibilities and promise of improved customer-service capabilities.

A review of the combined product line or combined facilities and capabilities is in order. Since the purpose of the acquisition was to expand the capabilities of one or both partners, the customer should know what the actual move means to him. He is certainly going to assume that it has a beneficial fiscal effect on his supplier. He is not interested, however, in knowing that his supplier is going to get richer, only in knowing what the supplier can do for him.

model letter F.1

Dear Customer:

As you know, April through June are the months of weddings. In this true   **(a)**
tradition ABC Inc. has joined together with PQR. We know that all the friends
of ABC will wish us well.

Until we can see you personally to advise you of the good things coming, we **(b)** want to take the opportunity of advising you that we intend to maintain ABC's present policies and methods of operation.

We will still carry the present lines of material, as well as add some new siding products.

Aluminum Siding: **(c)**

Wallmaster	Kaiser
Alcoa	Alside
AND THE NEW PQR LINE	

Roofing:

Bird	Johns-Manville

Asbestos:

Goldbond	Johns-Manville

We intend to have many of the same people contacting you. We also hope to have the same personnel handling your orders, as well as satisfying your other needs. We will give the same quality and service on which ABC built its reputation.

We are adding more profit lines, including the complete PQR Aluminum **(d)** Siding line, more ideas and more programs to help you build a bigger and more profitable business.

We hope this joining together helps make this and the coming years more **(e)** successful for each one of our customers.

Very truly yours,

ALTERNATE WORDING

(a) As one of our valued clients, we are sure you will be pleased to know that the ABC Organization is now merged into the PQR Corporation.

(b) This joining together of two highly reputable systems organizations, each recognized as leaders in their specialty fields, will enable us, jointly, to serve your needs even more completely than ever before.

(c) PQR offers you the most advanced systems solutions available in high-speed data control and retrieval systems, and all forms of automation input. The addition of ABC product lines makes available to you a broad line of graphic scheduling and visual control boards. Your needs, in every case, will be served by highly trained systems specialists who bring to you, at no extra charge whatsoever, the benefit of nearly three-quarters of a century of experience in solving problems for business, industry and government.

(d) Production and shipment will take place at Los Angeles for ABC products and at New York for PQR products. All accounting will be handled from New York.

(e) We look forward to the continuing opportunity of serving you.

2. NOTIFYING CUSTOMERS OF CHANGE IN CORPORATE NAME

A change in corporate name alone, without other changes in corporate identity or structure, is not a great change. It is a change that most managements choose to make because they feel that the new name will be more representative of the business of the company or may be easier to identify in advertising or promotion. The old company name still can remain in legal force, for various purposes, and receivables that come in under the old name can be honored.

Announcement of a change in name offers an opportunity to obtain promotional value without the appearance of promotion. To announce the change without taking advantage of the promotional opportunity afforded by the need for the announcement would be to lose some of the value of the change itself.

General Approach

Any change in corporate name must have been decided upon for a reason. The reason should be explained in marketing terms. Generally, the increased scope of business or technological coverage or activity is given as the reason for the change. Since the purpose of most changes in corporate name is to reflect the broadened scope of capability, the letter can provide a marketing emphasis that cannot be enjoyed in any other fashion.

The letter announcing the name change should be sent to all customers, current and active, former and inactive.

model letter F.2

Our new name:

ZYX CO.

Dear Customer:

For almost seventy years we have established our reputation for product quality   **(a)**
and reliability under the name, LMN Water Column & Gage Co. Your

enthusiastic acceptance enabled us to progress and diversify our lines, so that our original name no longer identifies what we manufacture and sell. We feel that our new name, ZYX CO. better describes our general operation without the limitations inherent in the old one.

We should like to express our appreciation to our customers throughout the **(b)** world, whose confidence has enabled us to grow. We will continue our efforts to warrant your patronage.

We would be pleased to forward our new catalog number 90-A to you, **(c)** upon request.

Please adjust your records to reflect our new name. (Naturally, we will continue **(d)** to answer to our former name, since there has been no corporate or management change.)

Very truly yours,

ALTERNATE WORDING

(a) For many years, you have been doing business with us under our old name. In recent years, we have enjoyed the benefits of new technologies, which we helped to develop, and have found that we require a new identity. We feel that our new name, ZYX Company, more accurately describes our operations than did our old name.

(b) It has been our fortunate experience to have had customers such as yourself who have consistently relied upon us to supply their needs. We hope and expect to justify your confidence in the future.

(c) Our expanded product line is completely described in a new, comprehensive catalog, which we will send to you upon request.

(c) Because our product line represents a diversity of products, we have issued new catalogs for each major product grouping. We believe that some or all of these lines may be of interest to you. The product groupings include:

(Give listing)

We will be pleased to send you copies of any or all of these catalogs.

(c) For the time being, our sales and technical literature will remain unchanged. Only our name has been changed.

(d) There has been no change of corporate or other personnel. You will still enjoy the service that you have been receiving from our current staff. Should you require any additional information or service to existing equipment, please do not hesitate to call on us at any time. We suggest you direct such requests to our sales department.

3. Notifying Customers of Change in Corporate Name due to Merger

As desired, the same announcement that goes to the general press, to the trade press and to other interested public media can be used in modified form or even in the same form for the announcement to customers, and even to suppliers. This is a sample of an announcement so modified. Among the many reasons for mergers, and consequent loss of corporate name, are some that are less than favorable to the merging company. If this is *not* the case, it should be pointed out that the merger will tend to be of positive value to the customer. In this particular announcement, such is the case.

General Approach

All corporate announcements are made in the name of the president or chief executive officer or by the president or chief executive officer. Here, the announcement cites the president and is sent out by the controller to the customers. Also, because one objective of the merger was apparently to supply the company with additional capital for necessary expansion, the expansion is explained first. This is a reassuring approach to the customer who must be made to feel that his source of supply is protected.

News of the merger is given in descriptive terms, indicating the new relationship with the acquiring company. Since the merger is presumably to be beneficial, it is not out of order to quote the president, although this is not wholly necessary and may be overstating the situation a bit. Also, the final paragraph, in which the size and scope of the business of the company is mentioned, may be omitted without loss of the basic idea. Should it be desired to cite the role of the company in its industry, this would serve as a suitable guiding paragraph.

model letter F.3

Dear Customer:

Mr. Harry Smith, president of the ABC Company, simultaneously announced   **(a)**
ABC Company's newly expanded engineering facilities and merger with XYZ & Company, Inc.

THE ENGINEERING EXPANSION

ABC announced new and larger quarters for their engineering department, quality control department and model shop.

The new quarters, located within the 100,000 sq. ft. ABC complex, offer expanded engineering facilities, newly designed quality control equipment and procedures and a completely equipped model shop for producing experimental prototypes.

THE MERGER

The ABC Company will operate as a subsidiary of XYZ & Co. and indicative **(b)** of its expanded operations will change its name to ABC Industries, Inc. with Mr. Harry Smith as president and director of engineering, Mr. Harry Jones as executive vice president of market development and sales planning, and Mr. Louis deLeon as executive vice president and treasurer.

Concerning the merger, Mr. Smith stated: **(c)**

> The ABC–XYZ merger will afford the ABC Company the opportunity to explore new vistas in systems and designs. We believe this new association will provide excellent support for future development and progress of not only the ABC Co. but the entire industry.

The ABC Company, now known as ABC Industries, Inc., was originally started in 1945 and is now the largest organization in the world devoted exclusively to the design and manufacture of laundry, dry cleaning and car wash coin meters.

Cordially,

ALTERNATE WORDING

(a) Mr. Harry Smith, president of the ABC Company, announces a merger of ABC Company with XYZ & Company, Inc.

(a) It is with pleasure that we are able to announce the merger of ABC Company with XYZ & Company, Inc. With this merger, we will be enabled to serve you more efficiently by means of the expanded production facilities that this merger will permit us to generate.

(b) The ABC Company will operate as a subsidiary of XYZ & Company and will change its name to ABC Industries, Inc., with all present personnel retaining their current responsibilities. No personnel changes or reductions are anticipated. Mr. Harry Smith will continue as president and director of engineering.

(c) We have chosen to take the steps of merging with a larger organization in order to obtain the benefits of financial strength that large size permits.

We believe that this association will provide the basis for future development and progress for both ABC Industries, Inc., as we will be known in the future, and the entire industry we have served and will continue to serve in the future.

4. NOTIFYING BANK OF CHANGE IN CORPORATE NAME DUE TO MERGER OR ACQUISITION

When one company is merged into or acquired by another, it no longer enjoys the same fiscal autonomy that it enjoyed as an independent corporation. The banking institutions with which it has done business must be notified and must be told what the names of the authorized signers of accounts will be.

General Approach

All mergers take place on a date that comprises the first day of business under the new fiscal arrangement. Whether the letter is sent in advance of the effective date or past the effective date makes no difference, provided no other complications can arise with either method of notification.

model letter F.4

Gentlemen:

Effective December 31, 19___, ABC Inc. was merged into XYZ Company, Inc. and became a division of XYZ Company, Inc. Therefore, will you please change the identity of our Webster accounts to reflect this fact.

All account numbers and authorized signers on all accounts of ABC Inc.   **(a)**
will remain the same.

Your cooperation in this matter will be appreciated.

Very truly yours,

ALTERNATE WORDING

(a) As soon as all necessary documents are in order, we shall forward them to you with a list of names of additional individuals who will be authorized to sign checks and to perform other business with the bank.

(a) The division accounts will retain their individual identities, but all business will be transacted under the name of the parent corporation. All account numbers and authorized signers on all accounts of ABC Inc. will remain the same.

5. NOTIFYING SUPPLIERS OF CHANGE IN CORPORATE POLICIES DUE TO MERGER OR ACQUISITION

All companies establish their own business policies. When one company is merged into or acquired by another, such policies are subject to review and change. When a change in policies involves relationships with suppliers, services, or other companies or agencies outside the new corporate structure, notification must be sent to avoid embarrassment to both the supplier and the company.

When, in the case of charge accounts and other personal services, changes are being made, the credit of the supplier is subject to being affected. Also, unless he is properly notified and assurance of such notification is obtained, he may have reason to believe that the policies of the old company are going to be continued by the new company. Therefore, any notification should be made by certified mail, with return receipt requested. In that way, the supplier is informed that he may not honor requests after the date of notification without running the risk of having his invoices refused.

General Approach

Notify the supplier of the change in corporate ownership and the effective date of the change in policy. Most frequently, the change in policy cannot be made exactly concurrent with the change in corporate status, but must follow by an amount of time deemed reasonable to allow the supplier to make necessary changes in his accounting procedures.

model letter F.5

Gentlemen:

Please be advised that PQR Inc. has been acquired by ABC Manufacturers Inc., 2 Main Street, Southfield, Michigan. (a)

Please close your account with PQR effective, April 21st, 19___.

(b)

Sincerely,

ALTERNATE WORDING

A sentence may be added, pursuant to the specific objective of the letter, as follows:

(a) Under our policies we do not maintain open charge accounts for our sales force, therefore no charges will be honored from persons making such charges on PQR's account.

A sentence may be added, as follows:

(b) Any charges made after that date must be reported immediately.

(b) No requests made by PQR personnel after that date should be filled without prior agreement from us.

6. NOTIFYING CUSTOMER OF CHANGE IN COMPANY OWNERSHIP AND OF HIS CONTINUING OBLIGATION TO PAY ALL OUTSTANDING INVOICES

Unfortunately, customers seem to sense the confusion that results when one company merges with another or when one company is purchased by another. It is not at all unusual for such accounts to fall behind because the confusion at both companies results in late invoicing to customers. In either situation, the customer has to be informed that he still has obligations, which he contracted in good faith with the former company and which were considered among the assets of the former company when it was merged into the present firm.

General Approach

Notice is given of the fact that the old company is now part of the new company, whether at the same address or at a different address. One of the first, if not the first, departments of the old company to be moved is the Accounting Department. Monies due are needed to keep both entities operating. It is appropriate, therefore, to indicate to the customer that the original company with which he did business is now part of another company with a different name.

The second paragraph informs the customer that he is to make his payments to the new office of the Accounts Receivable Department. To assure receipt of payment at the proper location, an envelope is enclosed. This is not merely a formality. The records of the customer show an old company name and an old company address. Without the enclosed envelope, their Accounts Payable Department may send their remittance to the old, wrong address, thus apparently delaying payment. The added delay may cause embarrassment if the time of the delay happens to coincide with a dunning notice.

model letter F.6

Gentlemen:

The LMN Industrial Division of PQR Corp. is now a part of the ABC Industries Inc. located at P. O. Box 100, Detroit, Michigan 49443.

Since the Accounts Receivable Ledgers have also now been transferred to **(a)** the Detroit office, payment for the subject charges can be sent in the returned enclosed postpaid envelope for immediate application to your account. We note your payment is now past due and we will expect your prompt remittance.

Very truly yours,

ALTERNATE WORDING

The last sentence of the second paragraph may be omitted, either if payment is not past due, if the customer has a good record of payment with the present company, or if it had a good record with the merged company. In other words, if the customer has not taken advantage of the changed situation, he should not be asked to perform in a manner in which he would not otherwise be expected to perform.

(a) All future correspondence concerning accounts receivable matters should be addressed to our Detroit office.

(a) All sales, service and financial matters for the former LMN Division of PQR Corp., will be handled in our Detroit office. The address of this office is: (Give address and telephone number; also include, if applicable, teletype number. Provide area codes and other address data.)

PENSIONS AND
EMPLOYEE BENEFITS

Pensions and Employee Benefits

Decisions concerning pension plans, employee benefits and other fringe benefits are not determined by the controller or treasurer; he just has to administer the programs approved by the board of directors. True enough, he is involved at the outset in determining the various costs involved in any programs, and he administers insurance and other financial aspects that may affect employees as a group. He also has the other function, even when there is an industrial relations department, of making certain that employees do receive the greatest value from the fringe benefits offered by his company. It is his responsibility to monitor the programs because, ultimately, they do involve the company's money.

1. CONDOLENCE LETTER WITH ENCLOSURE OF DEATH BENEFITS TO EMPLOYEE'S BENEFICIARY

The saddest part of a company officer's job is informing an employee's beneficiaries that the insurance paid either by the company or by the individual is serving the purpose intended. It is a most difficult letter to write because it combines a reiteration of the sad circumstances with the realization that preparation for this eventuality had been made.

General Approach

Since money is being transmitted, reference to this fact must be made, particularly so the bereaved will not read the letter and think it is only a letter of condolence.

It is well to state that the deceased, in a contributory program, had the foresight to think of his heirs. In a non-contributory program, it might be said that this was one of the reasons why the deceased felt that he had a welcome place with the company.

model letter G.1

Dear Mary:

It is with co-mingled feelings of gladness in the midst of our sorrow that we forward to you, as Paul's beneficiary, the enclosed check for $20,088.27. Insurance of any kind is the one thing we all buy with the fervent hope it will never be needed. However, since that cannot be, Mr. Nevin joins me in stating that we consider it a privilege to transmit this check, which is a tribute to Paul's foresight and care for his loved ones.

Paul was among the first to agree with the merits of a group distributor insurance **(a)** program. In part, we can say that his influence as an early participant made it easier to establish and maintain the program which has made this check possible. We hope that it will assist meaningfully during many future years of health and happiness, in fulfillment of a deeply felt mutual concern, on Paul's part and ours, for the comfort of his loved ones.

Sincerely,

ALTERNATE WORDING

(a) Paul was one of the earliest participants in the company insurance program. [Continue with the remainder of the paragraph.]

2. NOTICE OF APPOINTMENT OF PENSION FUND MANAGER

After many long negotiations, a pension fund manager will be selected to handle the pension funds of the company or a portion of the funds of the company. Selection involves many conversations, both face-to-face and by telephone, with many people during many meetings. Not at all unlikely, even the president of the company may become a party to the negotiations. Likewise, because interest by a union representing the bulk of the employees can be expected, union representatives may have sat in on the negotiations and participated in making arrangements of various types. This is natural since the establishment of a pension fund is a negotiable item in most contracts. The union leadership may be expected to have been involved in negotiations for a fund manager at a rather early stage and may even indicate their approval of the manager subsequently selected.

General Approach

The use of a first name in the salutation is to be expected. By the time agreement has been reached, negotiations might have stretched over a period of several months, or even longer, and relationships that were formal at first would have moved from the more formal to a more friendly and personal basis.

First, notify the person who has been selected as fund manager and inform him of his selection. Then tell him the conditions so that he may make suitable arrangements for the discussions of details that will take place later.

model letter G.2

Dear Dave:

I am pleased to advise you that we have selected your firm to manage a portion of the pension funds of our Company. The amount that we are planning to place with you for 19___ is approximately $2,500,000 and we have up to September 15, 19___ within which to pay out these funds.

Please call me, at your convenience, to arrange a meeting to discuss the procedures and legal documents that will be involved.

Needless to say, I am pleased that our decision was favorable and I look forward to a long and mutually satisfactory relationship with your organization.

Very truly yours,

3. NOTIFYING EMPLOYEES OF CHANGES IN STOCK OPTION PLAN OR OF INSTITUTION OF A STOCK OPTION PLAN

Informing employees of an intention on the part of management to institute a stock option plan is necesary to avoid problems that may result if the plan is "foisted" on the employees by vote of the shareholders or board of directors. The details of plans vary from company to company, so a letter that describes any particular plan would have to be modified to suit the circumstances. Generally, a letter such as this would be accompanied with a printed pamphlet describing the plan in detail. The letter serves as an outline of the principal features of the particular plan.

It is sometimes quite risky to expose a plan before approval of the Securities and Exchange Commission and the Internal Revenue Service, unless, as is usually the case, steps have already been taken that virtually assure acceptance by these governmental agencies. Premature exposure is worse than no plan at all, for if the government disapproves, the employees will feel cheated for having been offered something by the company which the company was not truly prepared to give. The company's relations with its employees would deteriorate.

General Approach

The idea behind an employee stock option plan is to encourage the employees to feel that they have a stake in the company.

It is presented as a benefit, although the benefit to the company will be as great as the benefit to the employees.

The circumstances under which the plan will be approved or presented for approval, as in this case, are given, either at the beginning of the letter or at the end of the letter, but not in the middle. The remainder of the letter is a series of descriptive excerpts of the plan.

Keeping the employees informed officially is far better than relying upon the "grapevine," with its questionable "information." By closing with a promise to give more information as soon as it is available is a means of forestalling rumors about company intentions.

The use of the president's name is a device. The letter will usually be written by the chief fiscal officer.

model letter G.3

Dear Fellow Employee:

This letter tells you about a plan for a new benefit for you, which will be presented to our stockholders for their approval at their Annual Meeting April 19, 19___.

We are also requesting the approval of the Securities and Exchange Commission and the Internal Revenue Service as is required in such matters. If the plan satisfies government requirements and if the stockholders approve, it will be effective July 1, 19___.

This proposed benefit is entitled "The ABC Company Employees' Investment Plan." In very general terms, it is as follows: eligible employees may invest amounts of 1%, 2%, 3%, or 4% of pay into an investment trust through payroll deductions. The Company would then contribute Company stock, valued at market value, and equal to 50% of the amount each employee has deducted from his pay. This contribution of stock by the Company would be placed in the trust for the individual until he becomes entitled to it under the procedures of the plan. An individual may, subject to plan restrictions, withdraw money from the plan at certain times.

Each person would elect to have his contributions invested in one or more of three types of funds:

1. A Guaranteed Principal Fund—Invested in government obligations, this fund would offer greatest protection to investment dollars.

2. A Diversified Equity Fund—The dollars in this fund would be invested in good quality stocks with emphasis on possible long-term growth.

3. The ABC Company Common Stock Fund—An employee could elect to invest up to a maximum of 50 percent of his contributions in this fund.

The "Employees' Investment Plan" is intended to provide the opportunity for every eligible employee to save money in a long-term program, which will be invested to provide opportunity for earnings under beneficial tax provisions. The Company stock contribution provides an opportunity for employees to actively participate in the ownership of the Company as stockholders.

This sketchy description is to let you know what is going on up to now. When **(a)** we receive approval some time before July 1st, you will get all the details so that you can decide what to do.

Cordially,

ALTERNATE WORDING

(a) Officials of unions with which the company has current contracts have been informed of the details of the plan and have indicated their approval. No part of the plan would adversely affect current benefits under these contracts.

(a) If approved, as we anticipate, the plan would be explained to you in detail by your union representative (foreman) at meetings to be held during working hours at various locations throughout the company.

(a) If approved, as we anticipate, the plan would be explained to you in detail by your supervisor, either individually or in small groups where you may ask questions. Such explanatory meetings will be held during working hours at convenient locations throughout the company offices and plants.

4. Notifying Employees of New Pension (or other benefit) Plan

Virtually all letters relating to employee benefits are signed by the senior corporate officers, but are written by the chief fiscal officer who must administer the plan. This is one more such letter.

Here, the officers announce an increase in benefits in their retirement plan as offered, free to the employees. Along with the letter, which would be sent to the employees at their homes, is the appropriate explanatory material detailing the new plan. In this case, because a plan already exists, an additional explanatory note is sent, comparing the old plan with the new plan.

Because the letter specifically indicates that the spouse must be named as a beneficiary, the letter must be sent to the employees' homes. This will generally assure knowledge of the plan by both husband and wife, since the letter comes in the regular mail. It should be addressed, however, only to the employee.

General Approach

Opening with "fellow employee" is trite, but true. Many employees resent this type of opening from senior corporate officers because they consider it condescending, but in a publicly held company, the board chairman and president are actually employees.

The first paragraph is straightforward and announces the purpose of the letter. The second sentence, however, assures the employee that he is receiving something without obligation on his part. Now he dares to read further.

The next two paragraphs explain the attached material, with the specific notation directed to the spouse to assure action on the part of the employee. If most of the company's employees are married males, they will not easily forget to make the necessary commitment once their wives are aware of the benefits.

Questions are always going to arise, so it is just good judgment to also notify the employees where to seek answers to their questions. The letter itself seems to state that only married employees can enjoy the benefits of the plan. Therefore, questions by unmarried employees are very likely to arise. They must be answered.

model letter G.4

Dear Fellow Employee:

We are happy to announce that the benefits provided by our Trusteed Retirement Plan were improved substantially, effective January 1, 19___. The entire cost of the added benefits will be paid by the Company.

You will find an explanation of the amended provisions in Sections 7 and 8 of the attached revised Booklet of Information. Examples are located in the back of the booklet. For your convenience, a concise detail of the changes made in the Plan, which compares its benefits before and after amended, is also attached.

Your attention is specifically directed to Section 8 (B) of the Booklet, which refers to the provisions of the Survivor's Benefit. Please note that your spouse must be your named beneficiary in order to have the option of electing to receive this benefit.

Should you have any questions concerning the Retirement Plan and the **(a)** newly added benefits, contact Mr. K. L. Jumel, Supervisor of Confidential Records and Payroll Accounting, at Extension 238.

Yours Sincerely,

ALTERNATE WORDING

(a) To make the necessary change, please ask your supervisor for the appropriate form, fill it out, and return it to your supervisor. He or she will forward it to the proper department. Your beneficiary change will take effect when you return the filled-in form to your supervisor.

CREDIT SITUATIONS
INVOLVING SUPPLIERS

Credit Situations Involving Suppliers

A particularly sensitive area is that in which your relationships with your suppliers concern the credit you have established or wish to establish. Instead of being in the comfortable situation of the creditor you are now in the situation of a debtor, under obligation to prove capability to pay, to meet payment dates and to insist upon good performance, particularly if a supplier is a contractor whose work is resold by your company.

All this involves far more than the amount of correspondence indicated here, with the most embarrassing of situations in which you find yourself usually taken care of by other than formal written means. A letter is necessary to provide proof of your effort, for instance, to notify a supplier that he has failed to perform to his promise or commitment. It is not desirable to tell him formally that you cannot pay on time and wish an extension, particularly when the letter you would write to that effect compromises your company by certifying to its poor credit position. Nevertheless, the group of letters shown here does cover a number of these more embarrassing situations, as well as some in which the supplier is at fault and must be notified as to his responsibilities.

1. REFUSING PAYMENT TO A SUPPLIER BECAUSE HE FAILED TO FULFILL HIS OBLIGATIONS UNDER A CONTRACT

Unfortunately, some contractors are unable, for a variety of reasons, to meet contractual obligations. When this happens, the company must notify them that it will not pay for services that have not been performed. Normally, this is a prelude to a negotiation in which that portion of the services actually rendered is paid for and the remaining part is contracted to another party. Should the cost of the second contract be higher for the unfulfilled work than was the first, the difference would be subtracted from the final settlement. This means that all negotiations have to start from a point of refusal to acknowledge any value received from a defaulting contractor. This letter does just that.

General Approach

Payments due are normally invoiced, so the first fiscal activity would take place when an invoice is received by the contracting company. In this case, the letter acknowledges receipt of the invoice from the supplier and of the work that was agreed to be performed.

The second paragraph indicates the circumstances that have led to the refusal to pay for completion of the first phase of the contract. It is possible that the original agreement included some provision for partial payment upon completion of each of several phases of the project. This seems to be the case in this letter. Under other circumstances, the refusal might be based upon the inability of the subcontractor (or supplier) to complete his work, yet he would argue that the work that was done was of value to the customer. Since, in this particular instance, the subcontractor is no longer in business, the obligation to pay is compounded by a variety of possible situations.

From the second paragraph, the third paragraph follows as a matter of logic. The company must make other arrangements for the work to be completed. The controller is asking the supplier to acknowledge this fact, either in writing or tacitly (by taking some other action).

The closing is courteous and invites further negotiations.

model letter H.1

Dear Tom:

Dave Hayes has referred to me your invoice No. 2477 dated August 6, 19___   **(a)**
covering the creation of complete parts file in the amount of $1,841.39.

Inasmuch as you were involved in our last year inventory you know full well   **(b)** that this Parts Bible is only the first preliminary step in determining our final inventory. Without the succeeding steps this first step is of no value to us whatsoever. Dave advises me that XYZ Data Company Inc. is no longer in business and cannot complete our inventory programming in full.

Under these circumstances I cannot authorize payment of your invoice since **(c)** the work which you have performed does not serve our purposes and cannot be utilized by such company as we will engage to do our inventory work for December 31, 19___. I hope you will understand our position and would be pleased to hear from you directly on this matter.

Yours very truly,

ALTERNATE WORDING

(a) On August 6, 19___, our company entered into a contract with your company to supply (items or service) with delivery (completion) scheduled by December 1 of that year. At your request, we extended the time allowed to complete performance by 30 days. We are now some 30 additional days beyond the extension and we have not received the merchandise (services).

(a) We have received your invoice No. 2477, dated August 6, 19___, for $800 for part payment of services performed to make repairs and modifications to our buildings and offices. Thus far, no work has been performed on our premises. The billing we have received covers the first 30 days of the contract, by which time certain obligations were required to have been performed by your company.

(b) The work required must be completed to be of any value to us. Without the succeeding steps, the preparation for the job is of no value. We do not have any reason to believe that your company is now, or ever will be, able to perform under the contract as originally agreed upon.

(c) Under these circumstances, my company must obtain the services of another contractor who will be able to complete the work we wish to have performed. I therefore cannot authorize payment of your invoice. I hope you will understand our position in this matter.

2. NOTIFYING A VENDOR OF YOUR INABILITY TO PAY ON TIME, REQUESTING AN EXTENSION

Cash flow is a problem with which all controllers and treasurers are acquainted, and one which vexes them constantly. Frequently it becomes necessary for a controller to ask for an extension of time for payment of obligations because his cash flow peaks during a busy season and ebbs at other times of the year, while his obligations are either level or seem, to him at least, to peak the opposite way. When this can no longer be handled by telephone—as a means of avoiding the embarrassment of committing such acknowledgment to written form—a letter is necessary.

This particular letter displays no embarrassment on the part of the writer. On the contrary, it seems to offer him an opportunity to promise improvement in the situation and to apologize for having inconvenienced his creditor. As worded, it also indicates that this is a thoroughly anticipated situation.

General Approach

Reference to the original written communication, here, to the company president, is made. Also acknowledged is the amount of the delinquency, confirming that the amount stated by the creditor is understood to be correct according to the records of the debtor. Of course, as might have been expected, the creditor's letter achieved its aim of obtaining some payment, if not all, as the amount of the remaining balance shows. In most situations, some attempt will be made by the debtor to satisfy the immediate requirements.

That the business is seasonal is, indeed, a reason for the delinquency, but the writer in this case makes no firm commitment that all payments will be made on time. If the situation as he foresees it indicates that such a promise can be made, it probably should. The recipient of this letter will easily see that he will likely still have money owed to him past the "busy season" unless further assurances are given.

The closing paragraph includes the apology and a promise to do better. It is a mollifying statement, which is definitely needed when a major creditor writes to the president of the company rather than directly to the controller.

model letter H.2

Dear Mr._____:

Our President has asked me to investigate and reply to your inquiry of May   **(a)**
19, 19___. The delinquent amount of $80,956.34 as stated in your letter is indeed
past due. At the time of this letter, we have made payment of all invoices up
through February 28, 19___, for the sum of approximately $25,000.00. The reason
for the degree of delinquency shown on our account is the low cash inflow at
present, due to the seasonal nature of our business. As we swing into the busier
part of our season, we will be experiencing a more favorable trend in our cash
flow and, therefore, should be able to reduce our delinquency.

We are sincerely sorry for the inconveniences we have caused you and will put   **(b)**
our best effort into improving the status of our account with your office.

Very truly yours,

ALTERNATE WORDING

(a) We have received your letter referring to a delinquency in our account in amount of $80,000. Upon receipt of your letter, we checked our records and found that we have reduced this amount to $25,000. At present, we are enjoying increased receipts from our current business, so we anticipate an early settlement of the outstanding balance.

(a) We have received your statement indicating that we have an amount still due you of $1800. If you will please check our original purchase order, we indicated that the billing for the work should be made to JKL Company, our client, and that acceptance of our purchase order and work to be performed was subject to that condition. It was also stated on the order that the excess amount of $1800 should not be remitted to us as a commission but should be credited to our outstanding balance at that time. This $1800 represents the amount of commission that is credited to us upon payment of your invoice by the JKL Company.

(b) We suggest that you debit this amount to JKL Company. We shall, however, make every effort to induce the JKL Company to make prompt payment to you in settlement of their obligation incurred through our agencies.

3. REFUSAL TO SUPPLY CREDIT INFORMATION

For any of a variety of reasons, a company may not desire to respond to a supplier's request for credit information. The company may be a subsidiary and may not have authority from the parent company to issue such information. It may even have only the right to refer the questioner to credit information previously made available for general use by the parent company. A company may wish to avoid filling out the necessary form, particularly if its credit data is already on file in a publicly available form, such as a Dun & Bradstreet summary. It may not be possible to supply sound financial data for a subsidiary because the accounting procedures may involve extensive intracompany fiscal transfers. For these purposes, an annual report may be eminently suitable.

In practice, the availability of credit information is not sufficient of itself to assure that a supplier will wish to open a credit account, nor is the lack of such information prejudicial to opening an account. Therefore, the amount or depth of detail is not necessarily truly significant. The general reputation of the company is by far the overriding consideration.

General Approach

Because dealings are on a company-to-company basis, the letter of refusal is addressed to the company, to the attention of the particular individual who requested the credit information.

The first paragraph acknowledges the request for information. It is not critical whether indication is given in this paragraph concerning the policy of the company relative to releasing such information. The reason for refusing to provide information may or may not be given. The closing provides an assurance that the credit of the writer's company is sufficiently sound to provide a good confidence factor.

model letter H.3

Gentlemen:

In reply to your recent request for a completed credit application and financial   **(a)**
statement, please be advised that it is not this company's policy to issue
such information.

(b)

To verify our credit status you may check us with Dun & Bradstreet; our bank,   **(c)**
XYZ Bank, Maspeth Branch, or our parent company, ABC & Company,
Corporate Office, Clifton, New Jersey.

We believe that the information you will ascertain will be satisfactory so that   **(d)**
you may open an account for us.

Yours very truly,

ALTERNATE WORDING

(a) We have your request for financial information for ABC Pipe Line Company. This company is a wholly owned subsidiary of ABC Corporation and is operated and financed by ABC Corporation in the same manner as ABC's other subsidiaries. Funds to finance the requirements of ABC Pipe Line Company in excess of funds generated internally are provided by the ABC Corporation.

(b) It is not our practice to furnish financial information for the subsidiary companies of ABC Corporation as a number of intercompany accounts are included in the financial statements of the subsidiaries and, as a result, their current financial position is distorted.

(c) Orange Pipe Line Company has purchased materials, supplies and services from a number of firms since its organization in 1936. A credit check with these firms will reveal that it has maintained a satisfactory credit relationship.

(c) You have our assurance that ABC Corporation plans to arrange for the necessary financing for the monies to pay invoices within the terms specified.

(d) For your information, I am enclosing a copy of ABC Corporation's most recent annual report.

(d) Please call me if you need any additional information concerning ABC Pipe Line Company. I believe you can rely on the information that you have in your files for ABC Corporation to ascertain the credit position of ABC Pipe Line Company.

4. Request to Supplier to Clarify and Correct Invoices Relating to Tax Charges

In the course of all business, errors in charges are made. This particular sample letter covers errors in taxes charged by a utility. It could be any excess charges or, for that matter, could concern a question as to why certain charges were not included. This type of letter would be written either as the result of an audit or as the result of routine checking of invoices rendered.

General Approach

Since the particular individual who would handle the matter is not known to the writer, the letter is addressed to the company, probably to the attention of the controller. The indefinite "he" is asked to review the account for the reasons stated.

Since a credit is being requested, the second paragraph carries the verification and indicates that it can be proved independently on the basis of the copies of the material enclosed as back-up proof. It was this original data that led to the need for a revision of charges in the first place. The amount of credit (or debit) is stated. As desired, the last sentence, suggesting a course of action, could be handled as a separate paragraph or serve as the first sentence of the closing paragraph.

The closing paragraph asks for a specific action to be taken.

model letter H.4

Gentlemen:

In reviewing our account with your company we have determined that we have been paying an excessive amount of Sales Tax based on your invoices.

The schedule of our invoices from you during the calendar year 19___ is attached herewith. Based on the schedule we are entitled to a credit in the amount of $667.87. We propose this credit be deducted from future payments.

If this meets with your approval please issue a credit memo to us for the appropriate amount.

Very truly yours,

5. Request for Confirmation of Delivery of Subcontracted Items (drop-shipped)

"Did you receive the materials that we drop-shipped to you?" is the subject of this inquiry. There is sometimes no way of confirming delivery of a drop-shipment except by protest several months later, when the customer receives his past-due invoice and finds that the product has not been received. Therefore, to avoid "surprises," the writer is asking for confirmation shortly after delivery was to have been completed and proof of acceptance would be in the hands of the accounts payable department, having cleared the customer's receiving, purchasing and accounting departments.

General Approach

The letter writer presumes that delivery took place, in the quantities indicated; it could be one or, as indicated, several thousands. To this, if the information is available to the writer, might be added the customer's order number or the writer's job number, if such would have appeared on the shipping and receiving documents.

Independent confirmation is desired and is so indicated in the second, rather straightforward paragraph. A request for confirmation is made simply, with a duplicate copy of the letter sent to the customer for him to sign as verification and agreement. This saves a lot of clerical work in trying to cross-reference the two letters: the request for confirmation and the confirming letter.

model letter H.5

Gentlemen:

According to our records, L&N Tool Corp. delivered to you on or about September 3rd 10,150 pieces of our Slide Extension No. 74-07 and 6,620 pieces of our Slide Extension No. 11-10622.

In connection with our internal audit procedures, we should like to have independent confirmation from you as to receipt of these quantities. Please indicate this confirmation by signing the enclosed copy of this letter and return to us. If you take exception to these quantities, please advise as to the quantity you actually received.

Yours very truly,

group I

SPECIAL SITUATIONS

Special Situations

Every company has some bits of work, information or material that are not sufficiently large in volume to justify handling as separate operations. These are the infrequent tasks that have to be performed but for which no organizational setup is justified. They go into a "Fibber McGee closet" of business. Every manager of the company has something of this sort assigned to him, and the fiscal officer is no exception.

This section covers some of these special situations. There is truly no way of formulating a complete listing because the list would become much too long and much too unrealistic for most controllers and treasurers. Therefore, the more common types of communications requirements are shown here.

1. Rejecting Request for Complimentary Advertising

Even though a company will establish an advertising budget, it seldom can anticipate the requests that will be made for complimentary advertising in school journals of all the schools in its immediate area; the various religious denominations that feel they have reason to believe they should obtain some support because one or more of their members is employed by the company; the professional journals of the societies of which various managers are members and whose dues are paid by the company; the local American Legion fund-raising event; the volunteer fire department Annual, and many, many more. The advertising department might handle these requests if they involve advertising, but they seldom do. So, in many companies, it is the financial executive who has responsibility because most of these requests fall into the category of charitable contributions.

It is quite necessary for a corporation, whose business is the making of profits for shareholders, to avoid a drain on its resources through charities. It is not in the business of supporting such charities and should refuse many more requests than it honors. This letter provides one such means of declining to make a contribution.

General Approach

Express sincere interest and desire to insert an ad, but make it quite clear that you would not be able to stay in business very long if, every time someone came to you with his hand out, you made a contribution.

model letter I.1

Dear Mr. Jones:

Thank you for thinking of our company in connection with your Annual Journal.

It would give us great pleasure to be able to advertise in your journal. As you   **(a)**
must appreciate, we receive many such requests as yours during the year. We
would like to be able to contribute to each one. To honor them, however, the
expense would entail a considerable cost on our part since to contribute to one
journal, we should, in all fairness, make contributions to all others that come
our way with as much reasonable claim as yours.

Under the circumstances, you will, we are sure, understand why we must
decline to advertise in your journal.

Very truly yours,

ALTERNATE WORDING

(a) It is our policy to place advertising only in journals that are related to our fields of activity. We find that even with this restriction, there are many fine journals to which we would like to be able to contribute. It thus becomes necessary for us to exercise considerable restraint in this regard.

(a) We would be pleased to make a contribution as a token of our feeling that the work of your group is of significant value to our employees and to the community of which we are a part. A check for $25 is enclosed.

2. DECLINING REQUEST FOR CHARITABLE CONTRIBUTION

Generally speaking, either of two sets of circumstances exist when the situation arises concerning the need for a controller to refuse to make a charitable contribution: first, there are no uncommitted funds available; second, a contribution has already been made to a united or consolidated fund of which the requesting organization is a participant. In the first instance, it is also possible that the company does not wish to make a contribution, but since it will have already committed its funds, whether or not it wishes to make a contribution, it cannot be done because the allocated budget would be exceeded.

As a matter of practice, some companies maintain a petty-cash account, which they add to each week (say $2, or even up to $10 per week), which they give, in cash form, to members of various religious orders who solicit funds on a canvassing basis. Whoever comes first gets the amount currently in the "kitty." Because many religious orders do not make mail solicitations, this covers a spectrum of otherwise worthwhile groups. This money is carefully accounted for, with the names and amounts given to each solicitor well recorded.

General Approach

The first letter is a general letter declining to contribute. It serves as an acknowledgment, particularly important for continuing good public relations with the community in which the company is located. Every request for funds should be acknowledged because ignoring the request may be construed as not considering the group and its members important to the local community. Also, some of the members of the soliciting group (if, for instance, it is a religious group) may be or may become employees. If they feel slighted by the company, unnecessary management problems may be created. The first paragraph also acknowledges the value of the work of the group.

The second paragraph tells why the request must be turned down.

The closing should not be too impersonal. The use of "sincerely" helps to dispel the feeling that the refusal is merely a matter of form. It is a more personal closing than "cordially" or "very truly yours."

The second letter covers a situation that arises quite frequently. Charitable organizations join with other groups in a general campaign for funds, dividing the proceeds among themselves in a predetermined fashion. However, the amounts collected in this manner are frequently insufficient to cover the needs of certain groups, so they solicit separately in addition. Little comment is required concerning this letter except to note that it leaves unsaid the not-so-obvious reasons for the consolidation of charitable contributions into the major consolidated funds, giving the responsibility back to the requesting organization and implying, properly, that a second, separate contribution is not in order.

model letter I.2a

Dear Mr._____:

I wish to acknowledge your request for a contribution to your very worthwhile organization. I am sure you fill an important need in our community and are very deserving of financial support.

Unfortunately, however, all of our funds available for this purpose have been committed for this year and we must regretfully decline your request.

Sincerely,

model letter I.2b

Dear Mr._____:

This will acknowledge your recent letter concerning a contribution to the   **(a)**
Southern California Chapter, National LMN Society. In years past, for reasons of which I am sure you are well aware, we consolidated most of our welfare donations into two major contributions, ABC Building Funds, Inc., and A.B.D. Through these groups we hope to reach all of the many deserving welfare and charitable organizations.

In reviewing the list of donees for the A.B.D. group, we find the LMN Society   **(b)**
to be one of the recipients. Inasmuch as our commitments for the year 19__ have

been expended in available contributions, we are regrettably unable to commit ourselves for an additional contribution above that supported in the A.B.D. allocation.

Meanwhile, our best wishes for the continuing success of your efforts on behalf of your very worthwhile organization.

Sincerely yours,

ALTERNATE WORDING

(a) Our company has operations in more than 20 locations across the country. As a result, we receive a great many requests for contributions toward the support of worthy causes.

(b) Since it is impossible for us to assist in every case where help is needed, we have confined our support to a limited number of organizations. Therefore, I am sorry to tell you that we will not be able to contribute toward the support of your fine work. We trust you will understand our position.

model letter I.2c

Dear_____:

Every year we receive numerous requests for assistance from various organizations. Due to our limited contributions budget we evaluate all requests with respect to our overall contributions program. Our evaluation is not an appraisal of the worthiness of any organization's endeavors but rather how we can most effectively distribute the limited amount of funds at our disposal.

I am sorry to inform you that we are unable to participate in your program this year.

Very truly yours,

3. REFUSING FINANCIAL PARTICIPATION IN BUSINESS OR PROFESSIONAL SOCIETY ACTIVITIES

Selling to an industry seems to open the floodgates to requests for funds to support that industry, to support the unions in that industry and, sometimes, to support some individual charities in which certain influential individuals are interested. If there is an industry association, there is likely to be some sort of program—usually non-profit on the face of it but supported by members of the industry for their eventual financial benefit—for promoting that particular industry in competition with other industries.

It seems almost impossible to meet all requests for funds; nobody has that much money, not even the large philanthropic funds. On top of the financial problem, supporting one industry may cause problems with another industry with which you do business. Consider, for instance, the plight of the manufacturer who sells valves to the "heating" industry and who finds himself under pressure to contribute to the fuel oil dealers when he also sells to natural gas equipment dealers and to manufacturers and dealers of electrical heating equipment. He simply cannot make a contribution to one without making a contribution to all three—or more. Nor can he contribute to a local fund-raising campaign at the risk of being obligated for 49 or more other local campaigns, all equally as deserving.

General Approach

It is appropriate to thank the requester for considering your company as a leader whose name they would like to have associated with their program. In the next breath, however, you indicate that contributing might become a source of embarrassment to you, and you don't want them to feel that they have placed you in a compromising position.

Reassure them of your continuing interest, especially since the person who writes the request is probably your customer. Your competitor's customer has already written him a letter asking for a contribution from him. At the end, firmly decline, but let them know that you do not want to close the door forever—although they should be astute enough to read that into the wording.

model letter I.3

Gentlemen:

Thank you for thinking of us in your fund drive for the PQR Institute New Equipment Development Program.

As a supplier to your industry, we are sympathetic to your aims and objectives.   **(a)**
However, since your request represents a single council, you can well imagine the situation we would find ourselves in if we would be called upon to contribute to each council throughout the country.

Of course, we still maintain our interest in serving members of your council, and the industry as a whole. Nevertheless, we have to consider our actions on a national scale, rather than only at the local level. Therefore, we shall have to decline to participate in your program at the present time.

Cordially,

Alternate Wording

(a) As a supplier to your industry, we are sympathetic to your aims and objectives. However, yours is only one of several hundred industries that we serve. You can well imagine the situation we would find ourselves in if we were called upon to contribute to each industry we sell our products to, especially since our products are sold on a rather wide scale.

4. Declining to Participate in Surveys or Projects not Germane to the Business of the Company

This was a letter declining to participate in this letter-book project. It was so well-written that it is included as an example of how to turn aside a request, however worthy, for participation in a project that requires effort, however little, but an effort the letter writer does not wish to make. The recipient of the request could easily ignore the request, but that would be very poor public relations. It is far better to notify the requester that you wish him well—but without your own participation.

There may be times when a request is answered, but it is going to be a rare occasion indeed. A letter of this sort precludes the need for ignoring outright those honorable requests that would not involve much time or effort but that are not considered proper activities for the company. The reaction of a person who sends a personal letter to a company only to have it ignored is never going to be favorable. If the letter is obviously a form letter, addressed only to a title, it can safely be ignored.

General Approach

First, refer to the request; second, indicate the magnitude of the task if all requests are to be answered; then indicate your refusal. The closing should always bid the writer well in his project.

model letter I.4

Dear Mr._____:

Your letter of January 20 to Mr. Hale, Controller of ABC Company, has been referred to me for consideration.

As I am sure you realize, ABC Company and its affiliates receive many requests from a variety of sources to participate in surveys and projects, and to complete questionnaires. Because of the time and expense involved, we must of necessity limit our participation in such activities even though a project in which we decline to participate may be very worthwhile.

We regret that we will not be participating in your project, but do take this opportunity to wish you every success with this undertaking.

Very truly yours,

5. Reply to Student Questionnaire

From time to time, students will send in questionnaires rather than letters asking for information that they plan to tabulate for use in college courses. The importance of these answers to the students should not be underestimated; the grades at the end of the course are determined by the quality of the results produced by these answers. However, student questionnaires can cause "headaches" and considerable extra work for those fiscal officers who would have to respond.

If the letter is personally typed and addressed specifically to an individual by name, it should be answered. Good public relations calls for that. But if the request comes in a form letter with a mimeographed questionnaire and is addressed to the title of the person who is to answer the questions, it is not proper to ignore the request completely, but it may be put aside. Such is apparently the situation that prevailed with this model letter. A personally typed and addressed letter deserves an immediate response, on the same basis as any personally addressed letter.

General Approach

Since the respondent had placed the letter and questionnaire in a "pigeonhole," he must apologize for the delay in answering. If this is not the case, the apology should be omitted.

The approach taken in this letter, particularly that of referring the student to highly regarded published works, is a suitable one. For one, it avoids the problems of having to explain the reasoning behind the responses. For another, it avoids having to provide complete explanations of new methods that have not yet reached the stage of being included in standard texts.

The writer should indicate, as a matter of form, that his answers represent only an opinion. In this particular letter, written by an official of a regulated public utility, mention is made that a short answer on a questionnaire could be misleading. In this instance, it could also be damaging without a suitable disclaimer, since the student may wish to compare the answers of other utility officials with the regulations governing accounting procedures as prescribed by the SEC, state law, and other agencies.

model letter I.5

Dear Mr._____:

Somehow your letter of February 4 got buried at the bottom of my pile. I had looked over the questionnaire at the time of receiving the letter and apologize for not having given you some answer at an earlier date. However, I am not sure any answers I can provide will be of much use, even if not too late.

Any simple answers to questions of the complexity of those in your questionnaire could be more misleading than revealing. Mr. John Carter of the XYZ Trust Company has written two very excellent books dealing with the problems of cost of capital and, of course, there are many others. The purpose for which you are determining cost of capital will in part dictate the method. In your questions 1-A and 1-B we would probably use a combination of factors you suggest for overall capital cost determination (e.g. rate case problems). A normalized cost based on weighted averages of past experiences of similar companies, tempered by current spot costs of capital, would seem to be a realistic approach. In regards to common equity, dividend yield plus estimated earnings growth rate is probably the most appropriate. So far as question 2 is concerned, one might use optimum capital ratios based on analysis of the industry, similar companies or capital objectives.

Frequency of determining cost of capital would seem to depend on the needs— e.g., a rate case, determination of financing requirements, or a decision to go ahead with or delay specific projects. You see, I just don't believe a simple answer to this questionnaire will provide meaningful results.

Again my apologies for the delay and I hope these few comments will be of some help to you.

Sincerely,

6. Rejecting Application for Employment

A request for employment, whether received in response to an ad placed in a newspaper or from a college student who has just received his BBA degree, calls for the controller to respond. Because the level of employment is one that would be handled by the Personnel department only after the employee is hired by the controller himself, the responsibility for answering such letters is best left to the executive who would actually select an applicant for employment. One never knows when someone ungraciously refused employment might later find work with the Internal Revenue Department, the SEC, a state or local tax agency, or even a company that will acquire the company so unkind to him only a few years earlier.

Quite realistically, the requirements of a particular position, even if advertised, are not satisfied by every applicant. A cost accountant may be required and the applicant may have no related experience. A specialist in executive remuneration may be called for, and so forth. Therefore, applicants will be turned down for good and valid reasons, even though eminently qualified in other specialties.

General Approach

Acknowledge the source of the inquiry, whether it is an ad or a direct application.

True or not, it is pleasant for the recipient of the refusal letter to feel that his application received thorough consideration. Certainly, it did receive sufficient consideration to enable the controller or his staff to select those applicants who provided the best "fit" for the job opening.

Since requirements do change, and because the controller and his staff do not know whether the background of the individual will be appropriate to the new requirements, it is not amiss, as indicated in the third paragraph, to promise reconsideration.

The final sentence is a gracious way of thanking the individual for responding. It is totally unnecessary to the message, particularly since many applicants seek only to find employment and have not specifically selected the one company from all others. They might have gone through a commercial register of some sort to find all companies in a given geographical area or all companies of a certain size, or may just have answered one ad along with 50 others. It is this final touch of graciousness that is most appealing—almost a lost art in letter-writing.

The closing is formal.

model letter I.6

Dear Mr._____:

Thank you for your resume in response to our ad in the New York Times.   **(a)**

Members of our staff have reviewed your application most carefully and although we were favorably impressed with your excellent qualifications, it is felt that   **(b)** our present opening is not commensurate with your particular background and experience. Therefore, we will not be able to consider you further at this time.

If our specific requirements should change in the future, we will again be in   **(c)** touch with you.

Your interest in our organization is greatly appreciated.

Very truly yours,

ALTERNATE WORDING

(a) Thank you for your letter and resume relative to a position with our company.

(b) . . . excellent qualifications, we do not currently have an opening commensurate with your . . .

(c) As is the case with any rapidly growing corporation, however, our staffing requirements change from time to time. For this reason we would like to retain your resume in our manpower register, and if a position corresponding to your background should develop, we will contact you at that time.

7. NOTIFICATION TO PUBLIC AUDITOR THAT HE IS NOW APPOINTED FOR THE NEW FISCAL YEAR

Appointment of a public auditor is required each year for the term of the fiscal year. This is a general legal requirement. For public companies, it is required by federal law and it is required that such action be approved by the shareholders of the company.

It may be assumed that such action is virtually automatic, provided there is no proxy fight that may relate to the manner of performing the annual audit, to the person or to the auditor.

General Approach

Action of shareholders is recorded and stands as a legal record, with the note a matter of record. Therefore, the letter to notify the auditor of his appointment or reappointment can be brief and to the point, without need for embellishment.

Coverage in the letter should definitely mention the name of the auditor, the company for which he is appointed and the term of the appointment. The name of the company is particularly important if more than one company is controlled or owned within a group or a conglomerate. As noted in the model letter, the date of the approval is also given.

The manner of closing is optional. If used, it should not be ambiguous. In the sample, the closing indicates the feeling of the writer that no further information is required and that he has conveyed all the necessary information.

Since it is likely that auditors and treasurers will be well known to each other, having worked together for a period of time, the use of "sincerely" may be appropriate. If the parties are not personally acquainted, a more formal closing should be used.

model letter I.7

Gentlemen:

We are pleased to inform you that Albert & Bennett has been elected auditor for ABC Terminals, Inc. for the 19___ calendar year. This action was taken at the annual meeting of the stockholders, today, April 15, 19___.

We trust this will be satisfactory.

Sincerely,

8. Objecting to Material that Appeared in a Trade Publication

From time to time, articles will appear in trade magazines that seem incomplete or erroneous to a controller or treasurer. When the nature of the information would tend to affect the fiscal affairs or corporate image of the company, it behooves the controller or treasurer to attempt to have a retraction printed, if that is called for, or a supplementary statement containing the additional facts that he presents.

Usually, the error on the part of the editor will have arisen because of a lack of cooperation of a sufficient number of influential and informed people in the field. The trade press is normally quite careful to assure a proper balance of information and to make certain that the various segments of the industry or industries to which they cater are not harmed. For this reason, when a letter of complaint is received, most trade publication editors will either print all or part of the letter or will provide a supplementary article relating to the error that appeared in the earlier issue of the publication.

Because of the manner in which various industries perform their accounting procedures, there is likely to be some difference of opinion concerning any article which quotes one method or which gives only a broad analysis without noting variations and aberrations. Such is the situation with this letter.

General Approach

The letter is addressed to the editor of the publication and cites the particular reference.

Following the reference and reason for writing, the author of the letter indicates the specific area with which he takes issue. This is necessary because the editor will not have read this article in some time—possibly more than a month—since it was committed to print. Also, the longer the article, the more difficult it would be for the editor to locate the point of reference. A direct quotation is helpful. Also helpful would be reference to the particular page and paragraph on which the statement at issue appeared.

Since the letter writer has taken upon himself the aspect of authority, he must cite his reason for questioning the editor—who is also an authority in his field. This, the writer has done. It matters little that this reference is to a utility accounting procedure; it would apply to a commercial or industrial situation of any type quite as well.

In the closing, the writer has asked the editor to explain himself. Should the situation have been more critical concerning the image of the corporation, he might have asked for a public explanation.

model letter I.8

Dear Editor:

Your August issue just hit my desk and I was much interested in your Special Report, "Start Solving Tomorrow's Problems Today." You did have one remark, however, that causes me enough concern to write you about it.

The statement is as follows: "As reported in EL&P's Top 100 Electric Utilities Report (June, 19___) rates of returns last year averaged 4.45% on net plant or, roughly, half of what utilities must pay in interest on the current bond issues for new plant." This caused me to review your Top 100 article, which I have saved, incidentally, and therein I find another paragraph which escaped me upon initial reading. This statement is, "Returns on net plant, given this year for the first time, ranged from a low of 1.86% (PQR Co.) to 7.19% (XYZ Co). The average was 4.46%."

A little checking revealed that you divided net plant into dividends declared to arrive at the quoted figure. It occurs to me that this calculation tends to distort to a great deal actual performance. You can see that older companies with stable situations expecting no growth would show a high return (because there would be no price appreciation anticipated and, consequently, a high payout ratio in lieu thereof), whereas, companies such as ours and other utilities situated in areas that are growing rapidly and, generally having a much lower percentage payout, would end up with a low return. I will admit that your example reflects the contrary but if you will examine the ten most favored companies, you will find that the payout ratios for these companies are more in the neighborhood of 50%. It isn't clear to me, therefore, exactly what you intended to show by this figure but I submit that it would tend to depreciate many companies which are from other standpoints some of the industry's best investment prospects.

I would appreciate a comment regarding your thinking in using these figures.

Very truly yours,

WHEN *NOT*
TO WRITE LETTERS

When Not to Write Letters

This section could also be entitled: "When to Avoid Making Commitments in Writing." For there are times when the written word constitutes a commitment—and there simply are times when a commitment cannot or should not be made.

The need to write business letters of any type tends to presuppose one of two possibilities: 1) that the letter is a form of contract in which agreements are formalized or are indicated as not being formalized, or 2) that the correspondence is intended to terminate a phase of a relationship or the total relationship itself.

However, there are times when neither of these two conditions should be permitted to prevail or when they simply will not exist. These comprise two major areas: 1) a negotiation in progress in which terms, conditions and obligations have not reached a point of agreement that can be safely committed to writing, or 2) a desire to avoid committing to writing the facts of a situation, which could be turned to the writer's disadvantage by the addressee.

Given these conditions, it is a time *not* to write, a time when direct personal contact is called for, either face-to-face with your respondent or by telephone. Within these limits, there are many potential situations that can arise. They concern dealings of all sorts and relationships in which you may be the recipient or the originator of the corresponding activity. Each type of situation is summarized below.

Contractual Aspects of Negotiations

Given a wide range of situations, the ones that controllers and treasurers will seldom commit to writing are those involving dealings with banks and those concerning loan negotiations. However, once the final agreement has been reached, the formal letter must be written in order to protect both parties. Nevertheless, while negotiations for a loan, line of credit or some similar financial arrangements are in progress, no formal communications will have very much positive meaning. Not until all negotiations have been completed and approved in an oral or verbal form can the final agreed-upon terms be set into print.

Of a like nature are negotiations that terminate in a document signed by both parties, such as a lease, a group insurance policy, etc. The only letters that would be exchanged would be (and then not in every case) ones that ask to open negotiations, and the final one, which covers the transmittal of the formal document between signatory parties. More probable is the opening of negotiations by a telephone call following either an earlier telephone call or a visit by one or both of the parties.

Confidential dealings involving corporate officers should never be committed to writing until the confidential nature of the matter is no longer essential to maintain. An example of this is the matter of dealing with a stock brokerage house for issuances of stocks, bonds or other corporate securities. In this instance, the need for avoiding letters is the basic need to maintain secrecy in order to avoid formalizing an agreement prior to the conclusions of negotiations—negotiations that may lead nowhere and the knowledge of which in the wrong hands could be less than advantageous to the company. However, under no conditions should letters be avoided when there exists the possibility that suspicion of special information may be given to particular favored individuals—the "insiders." The existence of a letter can avoid much embarrassment before the Securities and Exchange Commission. In other words, "timing" becomes important as to whether a certain bit of information or data should or should not be formalized.

Terminating a Relationship

It has been said frequently that it is impossible to turn down a reasonable request made face-to-face. Also, salesmen are, among others, always advised to visit their prospects to avoid the "no" response, which is so easy to give to a written request, or even to a phone request. A telephone request is easier to turn down than one made face-to-face, but harder than one made by letter. The letter provides the writer with an unparalleled opportunity, deliberate or not, to end a relationship.

Very seldom is a refusal to deal further followed by another request. Many types of letters simply do not have to be answered. They are their own answers to a prior negotiation.

If the person who wishes to terminate a phase or a relationship finds that he wants to hold the door ajar a little longer, he can use a letter as a means, but more often will find that a telephone call will do better. A letter can be used as a follow-up, indicating the nature of the conversation that took place, but the conversation and its ability to provide immediate feedback of information and attitudes provides more flexibility of negotiation than does a letter. Also, a letter may be construed as terminating a relationship that the writer would prefer to keep alive. In this situation, a direct conversation, face-to-face if that is possible, is the preferred method of communication.

NEGOTIATIONS IN PROGRESS

When a situation is still in flux, with negotiations taking place concerning such matters as bank loans, lines of credit, real estate dealings, insurance matters, etc., it is not appropriate to commit all matters to writing. In many of these cases, the resulting documentation may not require correspondence of any sort; signing of documents will comprise all the formal written matter and will take place in an office of one or more of the signatories. Only when it is necessary to transmit the formal documents to the attention of all parties should a letter be written, and that would be done for the purpose of establishing a transmittal or official date of acceptance of the document. It would contain no substantive material.

If dealings are in sensitive areas, as in the matter of labor negotiations or insurance coverage as employee fringe benefits, it is far better to avoid putting anything in writing that might fall into the hands of a not-so-disinterested third party. This is not because of any possible disadvantage but because the ultimate agreement may not resemble the matters discussed at earlier stages of negotiation. Although the information would not be used to hurt the company or its proposals, "wind" of activity might generate hopes and expectations that might not be proper and may not even have been anticipated by parties to the negotiations. In such instances, notes or minutes would serve the purpose but would represent the unofficial opinions of the parties, which they could review to determine if they should desire to continue along the lines of the prior discussions. In this case, a covering letter (which is all that might go into the official correspondence file) would simply call attention to the transmittal of the minutes or notes. The notes themselves would never be seen by others in the organization—as might occur if the correspondence file were routed—including secretaries and office boys, who are not privy to such information or data.

Avoid Committing Facts that Could Be Turned to Disadvantage

In every negotiating situation, particularly where the goodwill or corporate image of a company is involved, a conscious effort is generally made to keep private information away from prying eyes. Unfortunately, there are times when this is simply not possible because certain matters must be committed to writing, whether in letters or other correspondence form or merely in memorandum form. Yet, by avoiding putting everything in correspondence, it is possible to avoid embarrassment.

Particularly distressing to a controller or treasurer is the financial embarrassment when his cash position leaves him with an inability to meet his obligations, even within the long period of 90 days. He sometimes finds that he must ask for an extension of time in which to pay. Should other creditors find out that he is unable to pay a large debt in reasonable time, they may assume that the company's solvency is questionable and tend to press for payment of their receivables. It is well in such instances to make a plea for more time on a person-to-person basis with the controller at the creditor company. He will generally be more understanding than would the president of a smaller company, who has to handle his own credit matters and whose own company's future may depend upon the prompt payment of bills by his customers, or who has placed a large percentage of his business with a single company.

There are times when necessity forces a controller to commit his embarrassment to writing. Unfortunately, these "sometimes" occur when the company president is not truly aware of or does not wish to acknowledge the existence of a poor cash-flow situation. There is one letter in this book that covers such a situation, written because of pressure exerted by the company president. It would have been better if the controller had been able to resist this pressure. Having written the letter, he has committed his company to meeting future obligations, on a moral basis only, which he has no assurances that it can meet. On occasion, this type of letter may be requested by the president to be sent over his own signature, but the controller would be expected to write it.

Don't Put the Other Fellow on the Spot

In dealings with customers who have been prompt in payments over a long period of doing business, or of potential customers whose promise of business to come is possibly belied by their slow payments, the use of a letter, in any tone at all, could be, for all practical purposes, dunning, when asking for payment.

By your tone of voice over the telephone, for instance, you can convey some of the feeling that you could not put onto a sheet of chopped-up and rolled-out lumber: the impersonal letter. The person at the other end can plead his case, knowing that he will not be pilloried by having someone in his own organization call attention to the embarrassing financial position in which he finds himself as the custodian of corporate funds. You will also have been able to open the door to a negotiation in which each party can yield to the other sufficiently to enable each to claim that he has achieved some measure of his positive and favorable objective. It is easier to "let the other guy off the hook" by a pleasant tone of voice than by the same words committed to a letter.

Sometimes There Are Times When It Is Better Not to Write at All

In certain unusual or unique situations, it is sometimes better not to write in response to certain types of letters. The hope that a letter will establish improved corporate relations has to be weighed against the possible damage the letter might do or the possible annoyance it might generate in the future for the controller or treasurer and his company. Letters should be classified as coming from: legitimate sources, which have the right to expect time and effort to be expended in their behalf; and those sources that are simply nuisances. Every company gets its share of "crackpot" letters and, in this day of emphasis on environmental affairs, the number has increased. Worse still are those letters that come to controllers and treasurers from employees or ex-employees who have been terminated as a result of a financial decision to close an unprofitable operation because of the high cost of environmental-control facilities, which had to be built to meet the various laws. Many people blame these decisions on the "shenanigans" of the controllers (or "money men," as they call them), not upon the general managements or boards of directors.

Other crackpot letters come from people who ask for contributions for charities that are blatantly phoney. Many letters come from organizations that do not have tax-exempt status and to which a contribution would not be tax-deductible. These letter writers can get very nasty at times. Such letters should be carefully evaluated and, if found questionable, not answered at all. Answering such letters only leads to more and more such correspondence.

Letters from students that reflect a prying tone should not be answered. It is better to wait for a second letter than to open a correspondence with someone who is seeking information that might be damaging to the company.

A new type of annoyance has arisen of late. This is the "civil rights activist" who writes to every company to find out whether the company is doing what the activist believes constitutes a suitable job of providing employment to "minorities." Although this type of letter is generally addressed to the employment manager or even to the president, the controller may find himself in a position where the president has asked him to write a response. Also, in those instances where the controller also serves as the office manager, he may be charged with writing answers to all letters that cannot be directed to some other department.

If the letter comes from a reputable group, a response is in order. However, if there is any doubt, it is better to let the matter drop. If the president asks why, tell him that there are reservations concerning the matter of opening correspondence with a group that has not been mentioned favorably in the press, that has no standing in the community or that has already been known to have harassed other companies in your area. As a last resort, a suitable governmental agency can be contacted to learn whether the organization is, in fact, a properly constituted group to seek out such information. If this does not bring a response, the local newspaper may know. And, if the letter is at all abusive, the postal authorities should be notified. Once you answer such a letter, you lend standing to the group. They will use your letter to "blackmail" other companies.

Conclusion

The telephone is a potent tool of communication in the hands of a controller or treasurer. Just as in any medium that is reliant upon oral communication, it is capable of generating its own ambiguities, which only the formal written correspondence can clarify. It is a tool for interim negotiations, not a means of establishing anything that can be construed on a contractual basis. All telephone conversations or oral agreements, to have force of law or contract, have to be reduced to correspondence, which both parties can review and comment upon and which, at a later date, a third party can read and thoroughly concur or at least comprehend.

In other matters, no contact should be made. The less said, the better; nothing said, the best.